W9-BVM-518

YOUR *Perfect* NURSERY

YOUR *Perfect* NURSERY

A STEP-BY-STEP APPROACH TO CREATING THE NURSERY OF YOUR DREAMS

NAOMI COE

TILLER PRESS

New York London Toronto Sydney New Delhi

All nurseries in this book were designed by Naomi Coe of Little Crown Interiors unless otherwise noted. www.littlecrowninteriors.com

TILLER PRESS

An Imprint of Simon & Schuster, Inc.
1230 Avenue of the Americas, New York, NY 10020

First Tiller Press hardcover edition April 2021

TILLER PRESS and colophon are trademarks of Simon & Schuster, Inc.

For information about special discounts for bulk purchases, please contact Simon & Schuster Special Sales at 1-866-506-1949 or business@simonandschuster.com.
The Simon & Schuster Speakers Bureau can bring authors to your live event. For more information or to book an event, contact the Simon & Schuster Speakers Bureau at 1-866-248-3049 or visit our website at www.simonspeakers.com.

Interior design by Jennifer Chung

Safety by Adrien Coquet/The Noun Project

Manufactured in China

10 9 8 7 6 5 4 3 2 1

Library of Congress Cataloging-in-Publication Data

Names: Coe, Naomi, author.
Title: Your perfect nursery : a step-by-step approach to creating the nursery of your dreams / by Naomi Coe.
Description: First Tiller Press hardcover edition. | New York : Tiller Press, 2021. | Summary: "Design the safe, beautiful, functional nursery of your dreams with this inspiring and interactive step-by-step guide from renowned nursery interior designer and founder of Little Crown Interiors, Naomi Coe. Making room for baby has never looked so good"—Provided by publisher. Identifiers: LCCN 2020034589 (print) | LCCN 2020034590 (ebook) | ISBN 9781982152444 (hardcover) | ISBN 9781982152475 (ebook) | Subjects: LCSH: Nurseries—Decoration. | Classification: LCC NK2117.N87 C64 2021 (print) | LCC NK2117.N87 (ebook) | DDC 747.7/7083—dc23
LC record available at https://lccn.loc.gov/2020034589
LC ebook record available at https://lccn.loc.gov/2020034590

ISBN 978-1-9821-5244-4
ISBN 978-1-9821-5247-5 (ebook)

Table of Contents

Introduction

first of all, congrats!

You're bringing a new human into the world, throwing caution to the wind, and trying to figure out how on earth to create a nursery like the ones you've seen online or on social media. They look so perfect, don't they? The perfect crib, the immaculate and effortlessly organized changing table, and just the right amount of stuffed animals—how did they do it?

When I first started designing nurseries in 2007, there were only a handful of stores that sold nursery furniture. There were a very limited amount of brands selling crib bedding and rocking chairs, and there weren't a lot of style options. Customization was almost completely out of reach for the average consumer, and the idea of interior design seemed inaccessible to most people setting out to plan their nursery.

Now, more than a decade later, the nursery design industry has exploded! Pinterest, Instagram, and HGTV have made interior design more accessible than ever, and parents want to design a nursery just as amazing as any other room in the home.

The problem now is that there are *too many* options. Anyone looking to design a nursery will find thousands of aspirational images online and across social media, along with an onslaught of brands making all kinds of nursery products in every possible color, pattern, and style. Over the years, more furniture companies have launched baby furniture, more brands have been popping up that specialize in nursery décor, and the options for customization are much more accessible. And with sites like Etsy offering affordable one-of-a-kind options, the possibilities are literally endless.

Most of my interior design clients come to me confused, overwhelmed, and aimless. They want direction in this overly saturated market, a guide to help them navigate the entire process. It's easy to find inspiration photos of nurseries that you love, but then what? I see so many people with a proverbial pile of inspiration, but without the direction to know what to do with it. I've seen this situation create unnecessary stress during a time that should be fun and exciting!

My intention with this book is to give you the tools to create a beautiful and functional nursery. You'll learn my tips and tricks for planning, budgeting, shopping, safety, and styling so that you can create a loving, welcoming space for your new little one.

a little about me

I'm not your "typical" creative personality. I'm highly organized and live for a good spreadsheet (a strange thing to enjoy, I know), and in my free time, I also love learning about science, health, and technology. I like pineapple pizza, I collect rocks and minerals, and if you give me a house plant (preferably one that's very, very easy to care for), I'll be your best friend forever.

I grew up in a home where design was a part of almost everything. My father also went to art school and worked in design for years, and I have so many memories of watching him work—fixing things around the house, remodeling the bathroom, even making a life-size metal bust of my sister and her husband for their wedding—no joke! My artistic nature was always encouraged as a child, something I'm eternally grateful for as an adult. As soon as I finished my art degree, I went straight into an interior design program and knew right away that it was where I belonged.

My first job out of design school was at a small studio that specialized in nurseries and children's rooms. It was completely novel to me and I was intrigued by the idea of the added function that these rooms needed. Coupled with the expanded range of colors and patterns that clients were willing to explore and the warm and cozy emotions that went along with it, I was hooked. No beige sofas here! (Not that there's anything wrong with beige.) I started Little Crown Interiors in 2008, less than a year after I finished my design degree.

The nursery is an incredibly special space in the home where many memories will be made, and I believe that every family deserves to have a space that feels comfortable, safe, and beautiful. That's exactly what I set out to do with Little Crown Interiors, and here I am

more than a dozen years later with hundreds of projects under my belt, and ready to share everything with you!

my "conception" of this book

True to the spreadsheet-loving person I am, the first thing I did when I got engaged (after panicking because I had no idea how to plan a wedding) was search online for the best wedding planner book. There were lots to choose from, and I read the sample pages and reviews until I found the perfect one. It had a concise table of contents, checklists, tips, photos, and even a little folder in the back for receipts or pages I might tear out of magazines. It occurred to me one day while looking back at my own wedding planner book (which, by the way, I was ultimately unsatisfied with so I made my own in a binder), that so many of my clients would have benefited from something like it as they planned to welcome their new little ones. As with an engagement, there is a "protocol" when you find out you're pregnant: the first thing everyone does is buy a pile of books. And for good reason! Those books can teach you everything you need to know about pregnancy symptoms, how babies develop, how to make a childbirth plan, and newborn care. Some do mention the nursery: it's typically a small section with very little information. The internet is of even less help—it causes instant overwhelm and fatigue because information is found in small bits across tons of different websites, and sometimes it's conflicting.

This is all very unhelpful and just adds to

the overwhelm. In addition to the stress and anxiety caused by the transition into parenthood, you may also be dealing with nesting instincts, hormone changes, work changes, etc. Wanting to create a safe, beautiful, warm space for the life you'll be bringing into the world is perfectly normal and natural. I hope to give you the resources to do that here, all in one place.

After more than thirteen years designing nurseries and having my clients come to me with the same questions and concerns about budget, timeline, safety, organization, style, etc., I decided that I wanted to create a resource for parents *just* for the nursery. I wanted it to be beautiful and helpful—a book that inspires and relieves some of the stress and unknowns of creating this special space.

Now, I made a very intentional decision when naming this book. It's called *Your Perfect Nursery*, not *The Perfect Nursery*. No matter what social media might lead you to believe, there is no such thing as one perfect design. In every room of your home, but especially in the nursery, the goal is to create a space that you've infused with love. For some people that might be creating the perfect spot for reading and rocking. For others, it could be framing special family photographs and including Grandma's hand-knit blanket.

I have never been the type of designer to try to convince anyone out of something they love, even if I think it might look a bit strange or stick out in the overall design (as long as it's safe). I'm much more concerned with creating a space that my client will absolutely love. Be-

cause I want you to *love* your nursery. I want it to bring you serenity and joy. I want it to make you feel safe (and be safe).

This nursery is where you will make so many memories that you will cherish forever—of singing lullabies, watching them peacefully sleep, or even laughing out of sheer exhaustion—and you deserve to enjoy the process of creating that space.

You are the human being that will soon become a parent, or already are one. You will be caring for a child in this space. You will be up in the middle of the night soothing the baby's cries. You will be rocking them to sleep. I want to help you create a nursery that brings out your own inner child when you walk into it, a space that feels relaxing, and maybe even a little exciting. It's an extension of your home in the same way that your baby will be an extension of your family.

These next pages are full of inspiration, expert tips, and design lessons to guide you each step of the way. No matter what your style, budget, or needs, I know that with a little planning you can design *your* perfect nursery.

how to use this book

There is a lot of information in this book! I recommend starting from the beginning and making your way through in your own time. I've structured this book so that it follows the same step-by-step process that I use with my clients, from inspiration to installation—it's intuitive but also flexible. If you work better skipping around (not all brains learn the same way), that's fine too! Everything is organized in such a way that you can find what you need quickly and easily.

Designing a nursery (or any room) is quite the challenge. You will be researching, saving inspiration photos, budgeting, placing lots of orders, managing deliveries, etc. Make lists, keep folders, or create spreadsheets! Even if you're not the organized type, make sure you at least have a physical folder where you can store receipts, product registrations, instructions, and warranties. These are very important, especially for certain nursery items. For example, when you go to lower your crib mattress, you'll want to make sure you have the instructions handy. You may also need these documents in the event of a product recall. When in doubt, save it!

Throughout the book you will find worksheets, checklists, trackers, and space for jotting down ideas. I also highly encourage you to make notes, circle or highlight ideas that inspire you, or even tab some pages. If you just can't bring yourself to write in a book (which, to be honest, I probably wouldn't want to do either), you can always photocopy the worksheets and checklists and write on those.

safety disclaimer

Nursery safety is of utmost importance, and I would be remiss if I didn't mention it early on. Safety is my primary concern and I want to make sure that it is a big part of this book. To that end, in addition to a comprehensive Nursery Safety chapter, you will also find Safety First sidebars throughout the book to highlight common pitfalls and key concerns.

This book contains a lot of photos of nurseries, ideas, tips, and the like, but it's important to note that I am not a safety expert. While I have plenty of experience with nursery safety, I'm not trained as a baby-proofer and usually hire a third party to double check my clients' homes. The comprehensive chapter on Nursery Safety is based on all the knowledge I've gained from experience and research, but you should always do your own research and consult with a professional if needed.

I'm so excited to share my knowledge with you, and I hope that this book brings you excitement and joy!

Show me your nursery! Use hashtag #MyPerfectNursery to show me your special space!

CHAPTER 1

Getting Started

Get ready to take that first step! Just by opening this book, you're already making headway on your nursery design. Excited? Scared? Stressed? Enthusiastic? Yep, those are all appropriate feelings, and by jumping into this section I'm hoping we can bump up the excitement and remove some of that stress.

Parenthood is a huge milestone and I'm so glad to be a part of your journey. Often the trickiest part of designing a nursery is just getting started. Time and again I hear expecting parents say that they have some ideas, but just don't know where to start. I'm here to help you figure it out!

Left: Cuddle Clouds wall mural by Rebel Walls

get inspired

Gathering information and ideas is always a good first step when starting any design project. If you already know what you want, then you're ahead of the curve. Most expecting parents, however, aren't completely sure what they want or what they like. This is the first major roadblock that a lot of my clients run into. Even if you find a lot of inspiration photos and ideas that you like, it can be hard to know *why* you like them, and even harder to know how to translate inspiration into a design that will fit your space and your budget.

The best thing you can do in the beginning is to start saving inspiration. It wasn't that long ago that magazines and catalogs were the go-to for inspiration images. I used to keep binders full of ripped-out pages in plastic sleeves, organized by room with sticky notes calling out the specific details I liked. Nowadays we have the internet, which is where most people are finding inspiration. Pinterest, Instagram, and even just a regular old Google search can turn up thousands of images for you to peruse. Wherever you're finding inspiration, keep everything in a folder or use an online service like Pinterest to stay organized. Some people even just make a photo album on their phone and save screenshots—whatever works for you. Have fun with this part!

You may come across nursery photos with elements that are not generally considered safe, such as crib bumpers, fabric canopies, a crib under a window, etc. Keep in mind that some nurseries are photographed before the baby comes or when the baby is older, and some are specially styled. Some photos may also be older, and safety guidelines change frequently. It's important to do your safety research so you know what to look for and avoid. Skip to the Nursery Safety chapter to get a head start!

Right: This nursery was inspired by this bright and colorful artwork by Kerri Rosenthal.

sources of inspiration

Here are some easy places to look for nursery photos and ideas.

- Design Magazines
- Pregnancy Magazines
- Pinterest (try searches like "nursery design" or "modern nursery")
- Instagram (search specific tags like #bluenursery or #acryliccrib)
- Retailer Catalogs
- Parenting & Baby Blogs
- Google Images (search "nursery design" or "modern bohemian nursery")

After you've found some photos of nurseries that you like, take some time to look at each one and try to figure out *why* you like it. Does it have a calming color scheme? Do you like the furniture? Do you like the style of artwork? If you're still not sure, try covering up part of the image with your hand and see if your opinion changes. Sometimes looking at a smaller section of the room will help you zero in on the elements that you're drawn to.

Keep in mind that you don't have to only save nursery photos. In your search, you might stumble across an adult bedroom or living room that has elements you like. I've even had clients come to me with a photo of a dress, a wallpaper pattern, or a travel destination that they find inspiring. Additionally, don't even think about budget at this point. The purpose of this is to try to understand your style and preferences—we'll get to the budget part later. Use the same exercise as above to narrow down your preferences, even if the photos aren't of nurseries or appear to be out of your price range.

Right: Designed by Victoria Bell Design

anatomy of inspiration

Once you've gathered all your inspiration photos, pull a few of your favorite ones and do some dissection. What do you like? What don't you like? What commonalities do all your photos have?

This part can be challenging, especially if you're drawn to multiple styles. I've had clients send me inspiration images that look nothing alike, for example, a photo of a modern nursery with white walls and sleek furniture, and then another photo of a traditional nursery with baby pink and distressed furniture. The key here is to figure out what you are drawn to in each photo. Is there a color scheme in common? A lack of clutter? A feeling of cohesiveness? Or, maybe you find you're gravitating to individual items and not just the whole room. For example, do you like the window treatment style in the photo? A particular crib? The pairing of different materials? You get the idea.

If you're feeling frustrated and truly can't decide what you like, I recommend that you put all your inspiration away for a few days or even a week or two if you can. Don't look at it *at all*. I mean it, no peeking! Don't go looking around on Instagram or Pinterest either. Let the images you have already saved sit in your mind. Chances are, there will be one or two photos or products that just keep popping into your head. The items that your mind keeps coming back to are usually the ones that will lead you in the right direction.

wall treatments
Look for wallpaper, paneling or other wall details you like.

furniture type
Look for furniture finishes as well as styles.

textiles
It's good to know what textures and fabric types you like.

scale
Note the scale of items, like an oversize chandelier or large statement artwork.

contrast
Are you drawn to higher contrast images, or more monochromatic and subtle color palettes?

pattern
Stripes convey energy and fun while florals are whimsical. Take note of patterns you find yourself drawn to, regardless of their color.

themes
Saving lots of nautical photos? Images with giraffes? What thematic elements are you drawn to?

color
Note individual colors that appeal to you, not just overall color schemes, and also take note of color combinations.

metallics
Metallics can act as accent colors, or as neutrals. Do you prefer gold? Silver? Rose Gold?

Right: Nursery by Ashley Joy Houston. Mural design by Betty Larkin.

your seed item

Many times, when I'm working with clients, they will come to me with a single item they know they want to incorporate into the design. Sometimes it's a wallpaper pattern they fell in love with, other times it's just a crib or another piece of furniture. I've even had a client show me a photo of her tropical vacation that she wanted to base the whole nursery around. I call this the "seed" item—it's the item from which the rest of the design grows. Your seed item can be anything, big or small, that you know you want to have represented in the space. A color, an idea, an image, a piece of art, a piece of furniture—anything can serve as a jumping off point and will help you narrow down your options.

You may not find this item right away, but it's something to keep an eye out for while you're pulling and saving inspiration images. If you feel like you just aren't finding that one special item, no worries! It doesn't have to be super inspirational—sometimes your seed item is just the first item or idea that you decide on, even if it's just white walls, or where you want to put the crib.

In the next chapter, we'll dive further into your style and help you refine and understand the language to use to define your style based on your inspiration. But before we get into the details of that, let's shift gears for a moment and jump into some logistics!

nursery timeline

One of the biggest challenges in interior design is managing the timeline. There is a very specific way that most designers work to ensure that things come together in a timely manner. For a nursery, this matters even more because babies have a deadline all their own! This section will help you to understand the flow of the timing, but keep in mind that if things get off track, that's okay too. As long as you have the essentials, everything will fall into place.

Most of my clients will start thinking about the nursery when they find out the sex of the baby, or at around three to four months before the baby is due if they aren't finding out. However, I also have clients who get a late start, or want to wait until after the baby comes home to do the nursery. You certainly don't need a fully designed nursery immediately, but you will need certain essentials (like a safe place for baby to sleep, diapers, bottles, etc.) at the ready when baby comes home. You can read more about those essential items in the Nursery Checklist (page 14) and in the Budget chapter. But in general, I recommend allowing three to four months to complete a nursery project, from inspiration to installation!

Left: My client Jessi Malay fell in love with this floral wallpaper. We used it as our seed item and chose other items that coordinated with it.

set the foundation

First things first! Before you start buying or registering for anything, you'll want to nail down these five steps.

1 **Evaluate What You Have:** You may want to reuse the existing curtains, pull that vintage dresser out of storage, or use the hand-me-down blanket from Grandma. If there are items you already own that you want to use, it's good to know that up front so you can work them in.

2 **Identify a "Seed" Item:** Like I mentioned earlier, a "seed" item is an item or concept from which everything else grows. This can be a piece of art, a color scheme, or even an outfit. Pay attention to any inspiration items or photos that you keep coming back to or can't stop thinking about. If it keeps drawing you back, it might be the right choice for you!

3 **Create a Floor Plan:** This part can be tricky, but it's essential for a beautiful and functional nursery design. Don't worry, we'll get to the details in the Floor Plan chapter.

4 **Create a Checklist:** You might be surprised how many individual items are actually needed in a nursery. Use the Nursery Checklist on page 14 to stay organized. Use your floor plan to figure out what furniture items will fit and where, and that will also help determine what other items you will need.

5 **Set a Budget:** It's important to set a budget that you're truly comfortable with. Nursery items add up quickly and you'll want to make sure you don't end up stressed about money. Use the Nursery Checklist (page 14) to help add up projected costs, and read more specifics in the Budget chapter.

Left: My client already owned the window treatments and the wall art. We were able to use those items in the nursery and fill in everything else. Artwork over crib by Takashi Murakami.

start purchasing

Now that you've decided on a direction and budget and you've laid out the floor plan, it's time to have some fun (i.e., shop!) Start with the essentials and larger items, since those will inform your other design choices. Most of my clients start buying larger pieces, like furniture, somewhere around three to four months before the baby is born, but ultimately the timing is up to you. Bear in mind that some furniture can take up to sixteen weeks, especially if you're ordering something custom, and delays and back orders can occur as well. Due dates can also be unpredictable, so definitely order the essentials on the early side!

1 **Buy a Crib & Changing Table:** Most stores and online shops will have to order your crib and that can take anywhere from three to twelve weeks. Be sure to ask about stock and lead times so you can plan accordingly.

2 **Buy Your "Seed" Item:** Area rug? Artwork? Light fixture? Wallpaper? Whatever it is, if it's going to be the centerpiece of your design, you should have it in your hands as soon as possible so you can match other things to it.

3 **Buy Other Large Items:** Take care of ordering any other large or long-lead items, such as the glider or any other furniture.

4 **Buy the Necessities:** Make sure to purchase the basic things you will need, like a crib mattress, changing pad, diaper pail, etc. If you'd rather register for some of these items, you can wait a little longer.

Adding in accessories is always the best part of design! Use your imagination and play around with styling. Nursery by Ashley Joy Houston.

fill in with details

After some of your main items start to come in, you'll get a much better idea of how the space will feel. Some people choose to set things up as they come, and others prefer to do it all at once.

1 **Register:** Now that you have a good idea of the colors and themes that will be going into your space, you can register for gifts that fit your overall aesthetic.

2 **Finish the Design:** Start gathering up any remaining items to make your nursery complete, such as artwork, accessories, and décor.

3 **Choose the Paint Color:** It may seem counterintuitive to choose a paint color toward the end, but it's the easiest thing to manipulate. It's much easier to find the perfect artwork or fabric pattern and then match a paint color, than the opposite. You can have the general color in mind, but I suggest waiting to choose the exact hue until you have most of the other items. For more information about paint, see the Art, Décor & Walls chapter.

the last few things

1 **Evaluate & Refine:** Once you have most of your items and you've received gifts from your baby shower, you can plan how you want to put everything away. Evaluate the clothing you have and get some appropriately sized baby hangers. Figure out where you have empty spots and get some little storage bins to fit there. Once you have the baby and get into the groove of using the nursery, you may move things around a bit, and that's okay!

2 **Don't Worry:** Don't have everything in place? Crib shipment got delayed? Don't fret! If the baby comes before your nursery is ready, it's not the end of the world. For the first few months, you might end up using a bassinet or co-sleeper in your bedroom anyway, so it's okay if things aren't perfect in the nursery yet.

nursery checklist

Use this checklist to manage every detail of your nursery design, keep organized, stay within budget, and get inspired! Make sure to also note items you already own. There may be some items on this list that you don't want or need, and you may also want to add some items as well. This is just a guideline, so feel free to make it your own!

Custom dog portrait by Diane Rieger

item	description	price	ordered	arrived
Crib		$		
Conversion Kit		$		
Crib Mattress		$		
Changing Table		$		
Changing Tray		$		
Changing Pad		$		
Glider		$		
Ottoman		$		
Side Table		$		
Bookcase		$		
Toy Storage		$		

item	description	price	ordered	arrived
Ceiling Fixture		$		
Floor Lamp		$		
Table Lamp		$		
Artwork		$		
Mirror		$		
Wall Shelves		$		
Wall Hooks		$		
Area Rug		$		
Rug Pad		$		
Window Treatments		$		
Window Hardware		$		

item	description	price	ordered	arrived
Crib Bedding		$		
Changing Pad Covers		$		
Glider Pillow		$		
Glider Blanket		$		
Hanging Mobile		$		
Hamper		$		
Paint/Wall Color		$		
Wallpaper		$		

Notes

registry checklist

Most people sign up for a registry a month or two before the baby shower, but sometimes items for the nursery do end up on a baby registry. It's good to know in advance what items you want to purchase yourself, and what items you want to register for.

basic nursery items

Keep in mind that these items may overlap with your Nursery Checklist, but the items below are more commonly added to a registry and won't necessarily affect the design of the room. You can also choose to only register for non-nursery items if you want to purchase everything below yourself.

- ☐ Crib mattress
- ☐ Changing pad
- ☐ Blanket for glider
- ☐ Humidifier/vaporizer
- ☐ Air purifier

- ☐ Baby hangers
- ☐ Co-sleeper or bassinet
- ☐ Diaper and accessory organizer
- ☐ Diaper pail
- ☐ Night-light

health & safety

Some of these items aren't really necessary until the baby can pull up on things or crawl. Keep a close eye on them and add safety products as needed.

- ☐ Baby monitor
- ☐ Outlet protectors
- ☐ Smoke and carbon monoxide detectors

- ☐ Locks for cabinets and drawers
- ☐ Safety gates
- ☐ Earthquake putty

linens & décor

You may want to keep more design-oriented items off the registry, but you don't have to. If you find décor items that you like and are comfortable registering for, go ahead! Just keep in mind that you may not receive them all as gifts, so if anything is a core part of your design, I recommend purchasing it on your own.

☐ Crib sheets (3–4)   ☐ Hanging mobile

☐ Changing pad covers (3–4) ☐ Decorative objects

☐ Wall décor   ☐ Throw blanket

other registry items

There are a lot of other items you will need to add to your registry that aren't specifically nursery related, like bottles, diapers, swaddles, etc. Luckily, there are plenty of resources available online that give example checklists and shopping guides. You can check out GuguGuru.com or Babylist.com to start, and search around other sites as well. Ask family and friends for advice on their favorite products too!

CHAPTER 2

Defining Your Style

I t can be difficult to put your personal style into words, especially if you're not even sure what it is. Don't worry—you don't need to stick to a single style, but it is helpful to know the names of some popular styles so you can more easily search for items you like and refine your design.

Left: Butterfly Swell pattern designed by Holli Zollinger

what's your design style?

Hopefully by this point you have a good amount of inspiration images saved somewhere. If you're not quite sure what to do with them yet, that's okay! In this chapter, we're going to look at specific design styles and help you figure out where your tastes might fall. Before we delve into the different types of interior design styles, I want to say something that might sound a bit radical: being able to articulate your design style isn't actually *that* important.

Don't believe me? Think about your closet for a minute. I'm betting that you have pieces in multiple styles, patterns, and colors. You know what you like, what makes you feel good, what suits your body—and over the years you've accumulated and learned to pair pieces that are identifiably *you*. Maybe you have a few floral pieces with a bohemian vibe, but you also have some black and white staple pieces that are more structured and modern. Do you know what that style is called? Maybe. Does your taste even fall neatly into one category? Likely not. And, most importantly, does not knowing what your style is called stop you from building a wardrobe that you love? Not for a minute. The most important thing about your personal style is just that—it's personal. It's exactly the same for interior design. We are multidimensional beings and it's important to recognize that before we start talking about labels (so take them with a grain of salt). The nursery is such a special space in the home, and I encourage you to go with pieces that you love, first and foremost.

Knowing what styles you like and what the proper design terms are can help you when it comes to shopping and sourcing, but you do not have to stick to a single style for your nursery. Don't worry if your entire style doesn't fit into one consistent box, because most people are drawn to a variety of styles.

On the following pages, you will see twelve of the most popular design styles. Use them as a guideline to help you figure out what you like and what you want to aim for, but not as a hard and fast rule. Once you have a sense of what you gravitate toward, I'll walk you through how to use those styles in developing your own design ethos and making sure everything is balanced and cohesive.

modern

Modern design is all about clean lines and generally references items that are simple, refined, and high quality. Modern can be minimalist, but it doesn't necessarily have to be. When looking for modern décor, look for materials like acrylic, lacquer, and natural materials. Modern design is practical and functional, but also beautiful.

transitional

Transitional design is another one that's tricky to pin down. While based mostly in traditional design, transitional design aims to blend in, paring down classic elements using simpler fabrics and patterns, for example a traditional wing-backed reading chair upholstered in a classic neutral solid. The goal of a transitional space is to appear cohesive and relaxed, and it is generally not overly colorful or ornate.

traditional

Traditional design has classic lines and shapes. A traditional home will have a moderate amount of ornamentation, usually a few different patterns and lots of fabric and upholstery. Traditional design is also often seen in the architecture itself, such as detailed crown molding or ceiling medallions. Craftsmanship is highly valued and, if done right, traditional design can be timeless. French country and shabby chic are both examples of design styles that fall into the traditional category.

Designed by Lauren Elaine Interiors

scandinavian

Scandinavian design has also become much more popular in recent years due to the rise of minimalism. Scandinavian design uses light and unfinished woods and clean lines, but also curves and organic shapes. Natural materials and simple details bring warmth and comfort to a space. Colors are often subdued and soft with a lot of neutrals.

Design by Kristina Lynne

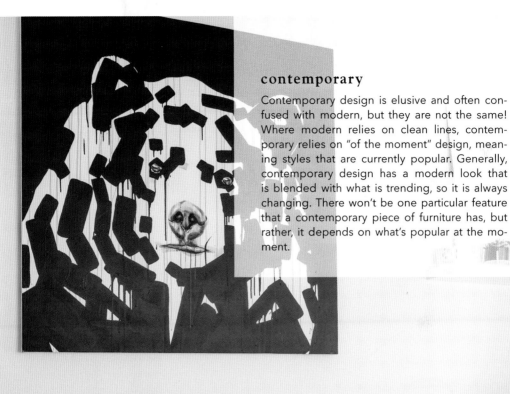

contemporary

Contemporary design is elusive and often confused with modern, but they are not the same! Where modern relies on clean lines, contemporary relies on "of the moment" design, meaning styles that are currently popular. Generally, contemporary design has a modern look that is blended with what is trending, so it is always changing. There won't be one particular feature that a contemporary piece of furniture has, but rather, it depends on what's popular at the moment.

Bear artwork by Chad Hasegawa

mid-century modern

Mid-century modern is perhaps the most recognizable design style. There are so many available options with entire brands selling mainly this style. Mid-century modern first appeared in the 1950s and 1960s, and was popularized again after the release of *Mad Men*. Mid-century modern uses warm wood tones, retro colors like orange and avocado green, and clean lines. It's so versatile that it looks good in almost every space.

bohemian

Also sometimes referred to as "eclectic," bohemian design has been incredibly popular over the past several years, and for good reason! This style focuses on items that have rich character and a story behind them. Bohemian décor usually involves items with a global feel, as if each piece were purchased while traveling the world. Often very colorful, bohemian décor is not subtle, uses a heavy-hand for texture, and promotes lots of layering.

LOVE YOU BABE

Design by Nikki Anderson

coastal

Coastal design is one of the easiest to identify because it often includes thematic elements. Coastal design is most often seen in coastal areas, but that doesn't mean you can't use it if you're far away from water! Coastal design is beachy, casual, and uses lots of light woods, blue hues, and touches of beach-themed items like coral or shells.

farmhouse rustic

The farmhouse style was made wildly popular by design powerhouse Joanna Gaines, and it features a mix of rustic décor, natural materials, and weathered finishes. This includes things like shiplap, recycled wood, exposed brick, and warm colors. The farmhouse style focuses on family, and it favors communal spaces, open layouts, and positive themed décor.

dream big
little one

Design by Dania Freudenburg of The Sycamore House

hollywood regency

If you love glamour and bling, this might be your style! Hollywood Regency was most popular in the 1940s through the 1960s, largely due to designer Dorothy Draper. It combines styles from the past, like Art Deco, with modern sophistication, and a dash of glitz and glamour from the old-fashioned movie star era. Crystal, mirrored furniture, black lacquer, and pops of bright color are all mainstays of Hollywood Regency.

develop your style

In Chapter 1, we talked about what a seed item is, and how it can be used as the inspiration for your whole design. Now we can get into a bit more detail about how to use that item, along with your preferences and style, to build a balanced and cohesive nursery.

1 **Start with the Seed:** Hopefully you've chosen a seed item by now, but if not, that's okay too! You can certainly build your design from a color scheme, theme, pattern, or style—it doesn't have to be a particular item. You don't even have to use the seed item in the room. You can still pull colors and themes from a seed item, even if it's not a décor piece. This means you can choose literally anything—a piece of clothing, a photo of a home, even a movie or TV show.

2 **Pick and Choose:** Here's where you get to have some fun. Most of the nurseries you will see are not a singular style, but rather incorporate elements of multiple styles. You can use the design styles as a framework to help you understand what you like, but there's no rule that says you can't select pieces you love from other styles. For example, you can choose a modern crib and pair it with a traditional wallpaper. At this stage, you can choose items you like in the styles you like. Don't be afraid to double up, for example, choosing two wallpaper patterns, or two rugs. Options are okay! Nothing is set in stone yet.

3 **Balance Your Design:** In order to create a cohesive design, you will need to blend and balance the various style elements you choose. This is where those options you chose can really come into play. Because while it's perfectly okay to mix and match styles, you don't want a room that's almost entirely one style, but then has a seemingly misplaced item from another style. The same goes for any color, texture, or pattern, even within a single style. For example, let's say you're going to use two main styles: modern and traditional. You'll want to use elements of both in a few different areas of the room so you don't end up with half the room looking modern and half looking traditional. If you choose a traditional dresser, maybe add a modern mirror above it, or modern knobs. For a modern glider, add a traditional throw pillow or lamp on the side table. If you have modern pieces on one wall, make sure there is something modern on the opposite wall. Same rules apply if you have more than two styles in the room. The goal is balance.

Left: Design by Frances Lubarsky of Designed by Fran

style & preferences

Use the area below to write down any notes you have on your style, preferences, likes, and dislikes. You can also keep track of specific products, websites, stores, items recommended by friends, as well as your budget and timeline.

style notes

Styles:

_____

_____

_____

_____

Colors:

_____

_____

_____

_____

Walls:

_____

_____

_____

_____

Patterns:

_____

_____

_____

_____

Furniture:

_____

_____

_____

_____

Windows:

_____

_____

_____

_____

Floors:

_____

_____

_____

_____

Themes:

_____

_____

_____

_____

Textures:

_____

_____

_____

_____

CHAPTER 3

Nursery Safety

Nursery safety is the most important element of any nursery design. Just because it looks good, doesn't mean it's safe. But safety can absolutely be beautiful! This section may feel a bit scary, but it's important to arm yourself with information—the more prepared you are, the better.

I'm just going to put this out there: Talking about nursery safety can be scary. There are so many articles, recall notices, and cautionary tales regarding safety that it can be overwhelming. The reason I've chosen to include it so early on in the book is because safety will inform the rest of your design decision making. Knowing safety rules before you get too far into the design is helpful because it will prevent you from getting your heart set on something that's not realistic, and also help you narrow down options. For example, when you're shopping for artwork to go over your crib, you'll know to avoid anything heavy or that has glass.

If you already find yourself feeling anxious or apprehensive about safety, you can save this chapter for later, or read it in small doses. However, don't leave it out entirely—it's very important and will save you the headache later of trying to baby-proof a room full of unsafe items!

my #1 safety tip

Before we get into the specifics of baby-proofing, there is one very simple and effective mantra every parent can follow: Pay attention. And I want you to pay attention in two ways: First, pay attention to how your baby moves, how they sleep, how quickly they are learning. In addition, watch their behavior: Are they curious or do they tend to leave things alone? Are there certain areas in your home they are drawn to? Certain textures, colors, or objects? Every baby will have their own energy, personality, habits, and curiosities, and your baby's tendencies will give you insight into what you might need to stay ahead of, safety-wise.

For example, the nursery of a baby who is a natural explorer might benefit from less clutter for them to get into, and additional safety measures such as a second baby monitor to see other parts of the room once they are more mobile. Pay attention to your baby's patterns and be aware that those patterns may change.

Paying attention also means supervising your baby at all times. You've undoubtedly heard stories that begin with, "I turned around for two seconds and . . ." This is important even when your baby is a newborn. It's easy to take comfort in the fact that as a newborn, your baby won't be able to climb out of the crib or knock things over, so you may end up putting things in the nursery that could become a problem later. Your baby could learn a new behavior or skill very quickly, sometimes overnight, so constant supervision is key.

baby monitors

One of the easiest ways to pay attention to your baby, especially how they behave when you're not around, is with a baby monitor—something every nursery should have. In addition to giving you the ability to keep an eye on your baby, they provide the peace of mind all new parents need. You can rest easy (at least for a few hours) knowing that the monitor will alert you to any issues. There are countless monitors on the market, ranging from more traditional one-way radio styles to models that include both audio and visual components. There are even high-tech monitors that can monitor baby's breathing and heart rate!

While audio-only monitors are still available, I strongly recommend models with both audio and video monitoring. In addition to knowing when they are crying or waking up, the added visual component will also show you how they move. You'll be able to see when they start rolling around, when they start pulling up on the crib rails, and if they try to climb out of the crib.

The best angle for viewing is to have the monitor mounted on the wall above the crib with the camera facing straight down. This will give you a direct view into the crib with no obstructions. The height above the crib may change a bit depending on the manufacturer, so make sure to follow the instructions. Some monitors don't come with an option to mount them on the wall, so you may need to play around with ways to get the best angle. There are also separate wall mounts you can purchase.

Your baby monitor will also likely have a cord, so please refer to the next section on Electrical Safety before installing.

SAFETY FIRST

You may notice that a lot of nurseries in this book don't have baby monitors. That's because I often photograph my clients' nurseries before the baby is born, and sometimes even before the baby shower, so they don't have a monitor installed yet. This doesn't mean you don't need one—you definitely do!

---

electrical safety

A modern nursery is guaranteed to have items that require electricity, like the baby monitor, table or floor lamps, humidifiers, a wipes warmer, or even your glider (some have a plug for a USB charger or motorized recliner). Most items will need to be plugged in and will have a cord, all of which need special safety consideration.

Outlets: Your room will have multiple electrical outlets, which can be a hazard in the event that a mobile baby tries to stick something into them. Use spring-loaded outlet protectors in every outlet that isn't being used, even if they are behind furniture. If you have a power strip, use a power strip cover. Depending on the layout of your room, the wall outlets might not be in the perfect place. For example, if you need

---

Left: Baby monitors can also be standing rather than mounted on the wall. Design by Mackenzie Horan Beuttenmuller.

to plug something in, but the nearest outlet is several feet away, you may end up with a visible and accessible cord. Try to keep these to an absolute minimum, and read the next section for how to safely handle cords.

Cords: Cords are dangerous not only because they carry electricity, but also because they pose a strangulation risk. If you are using an item that has a cord, place it away from the crib. For example, if you have a baby monitor with a cord, make sure that cord is not reachable from the crib by at least three feet. Some parents place the monitor on the crib rail because it provides a good angle, but this is a safety hazard. Instead, choose a monitor that can be mounted on the wall or has a wider lens so it can be placed farther from the crib. Ideally, all cords should be tacked to the wall or baseboards with a wire cover or tucked and secured behind furniture.

Make sure any and all cords are completely inaccessible and use wire covers or secure them to baseboards if needed.

smoke detectors

You'll want to make sure that the nursery has both a fully functional smoke detector and a carbon monoxide detector. If you haven't tested yours in a while, find the manufacturer's manual and follow the instructions to test each unit. If you're renting, you should be able to find the serial number on the device and look it up online, or you can check with your landlord.

crib safety

It may be surprising that there are so many safety concerns with cribs, but unfortunately even if the crib itself is high quality and well built, there may still be concerns depending on how it's assembled, where it's placed, and what items are put in it. Many of the tips below may also pertain to bassinets, portable sleepers, and play yards.

shopping for the crib

Make sure that your model meets the most current safety standards. You may also want to check if the manufacturer has had any recent product recalls. You can find crib regulations and recall information at www.CPSC.gov. Never, I repeat *never*, use a drop-side crib. They do not meet the current safety standards, and they haven't since 2011, but you may come across one if you are borrowing a crib or considering a hand-me-down.

assembling the crib

Always follow the instructions exactly, and *never* cut corners when assembling. Keep all the manuals and warranties and fill out the registration card if there is one so you will be notified of any recalls or issues. If you notice any missing parts, even just a single screw, contact the manufacturer and do not place the baby in the crib until a replacement has arrived.

For newborns, assemble the crib with the mattress at the highest setting. When the baby starts to move around a lot or can sit, drop the mattress height down. If you're not sure when to drop the mattress, talk to your doctor or a safety professional.

Top: My client Melissa Molinaro wanted a crib with acrylic for its modern look.

crib placement

Cribs should not be placed under a window for many reasons:

- The sun that comes through the window can actually sunburn the baby or cause overheating.
- In colder weather, it can expose the baby to drafts.
- There is a risk of the baby opening the window once they are old enough to reach up.
- It's not safe to have hanging window cords near the crib.
- There is the risk of breaking glass, especially in locations at risk for earthquakes or hurricanes.

Cribs also should not be placed so close to another piece of furniture that a more mobile baby or a toddler can use to help them climb out of the crib, or fall on if they manage to get out. When your baby is able to move around and pull up in the crib, you should also pull the crib away from the wall several inches so they don't get stuck between the crib and the wall.

If your room has a radiator, floor vents or baseboard heaters, you'll want to avoid placing the crib near those as well so there isn't an issue with temperature control in the crib.

Crib Décor: There should be *no* décor items reachable from the crib, for example crib canopies or low-hanging mobiles. If you're using a crib mobile, hang it from the ceiling with plenty of distance between the crib and the bottom of the mobile. As your baby ages, you may have to rearrange décor to keep it out of arms reach.

The Mattress: The crib mattress should be firm and fit in the crib snugly with no gaps or spaces around the edges. Most crib mattresses are standard size, but you should always double check that your mattress fits snugly in your crib.

Maintenance: Over time, your crib might start to show signs of wear. If anything appears to be broken or no longer seems structurally sound (such as a loose crib slat), call the manufacturer. Do not attempt any repairs yourself! Any tampering (even well-meaning makeshift repairs) will nullify the warranty. Contact the manufacturer and remove your baby from the crib until it is repaired or replaced.

Feeling overwhelmed by all the nursery safety information? Find childproofing professionals in your area at www.iafcs.org.

Left: When hanging a mobile above a crib, make sure it is fully secured and hung plenty high enough so baby can't reach it.

sleep safety

Newborns can sleep up to seventeen hours a day! Some of that time will be in the crib, bassinet, or co-sleeper, but it could also be in the car seat, moses basket, or even just while you're holding them. Because they spend such a large amount of time asleep, it's important to pay attention to sleep safety, no matter where they are sleeping, or what time of day or night. The main safety issue with sleeping is the baby's access to air and preventing SIDS (Sudden Infant Death Syndrome).

Newborns should always be placed on their back to sleep in a crib or bassinet. Do not place any other items in the crib including blankets, pillows, stuffed animals, or sleep positioners (all of which are a suffocation hazard).

Some parents like to have the baby sleep in their bedroom for the first several months. You can do this with a bassinet or co-sleeper, or even put the crib in a safe spot in the bedroom. However, it is not recommended that you sleep with the baby in bed with you, as this is a suffocation hazard.

Crib Bumpers: Crib bumpers are used less and less these days because of increasing safety concerns, but they are still available and you may see them in a lot of your inspiration photos. Crib bumpers should only be used for decoration and should never be in the crib with the baby. When the baby is a newborn, bumpers can be a suffocation hazard. When the baby is older, they can stand or climb on the bumper, posing a fall risk. There are some breathable and mesh options available if you feel you need something between the baby and the crib rails.

Right: Ceiling fans can help reduce risk of SIDS. Design by Jamie Baslow.

window safety

Window treatments are one of the trickiest things to deal with in nursery design. Window treatments are expensive, and many parents opt to use what they already have—which, while cost effective, may not be the safest option. No matter what type of window treatments you have, make sure they are very well secured when installed (that way, if the baby is able to pull on them, they won't fall down).

Shades: Any type of shade, such as a roman shade, roll-down, or blind, will likely have some type of cord system. Just like electrical cords, window treatment cords also pose a strangulation hazard, but they may additionally have a cord system that has tension (meaning when you pull the cord, it will have upward tension). This can make it much more dangerous for a child to get stuck. Go for cordless options if at all possible. Keep in mind that even if you tie the cords up with cleats high on the wall, children can still climb on furniture to access them.

Curtains: Most curtains don't have cords, but some might if they are on a traverse system. Again, go cordless! Make sure that curtains are hung securely so if a child pulls on them, they won't come off the wall.

Window Locks: Once your child is big enough to climb out of the crib, you might want to look into window locks, especially if your nursery isn't on the first floor, and definitely if you have an adventurous or curious child.

artwork & décor

You will likely be hanging artwork and/or other items on the walls in your nursery. Even the safety of these things needs to be considered!

Art Over the Crib: Don't hang anything with glass in it over the crib, such as a framed piece of art or a mirror. If it were to fall, you definitely don't want broken glass in the crib. Anything that you do hang, no matter how lightweight, should be fully secured to the wall. When in doubt, more secure is always better. If you do want to hang a framed print, replace the glass with plexiglass (you can order custom cut acrylic online). Always test the safety of things as well by trying to knock them off the wall yourself from different angles. It shouldn't budge!

Décor Over the Changing Table: While it might not seem like an issue to hang something over the changing table, remember that your baby may flail around and kick while they are being changed. If you have anything on the wall that might get knocked loose, that can be a safety hazard. I often use mirrors over the changing table in a lot of my designs, and we always make sure they are heavily secured.

Left: A wall mural is a totally safe way to achieve a statement look behind the crib without hanging anything on the wall! Mural by Wall Art by Allyson.

storage safety

You may end up purchasing some additional small storage pieces, like a toy box or storage bench, that provide closed storage. This also applies to things like window seats that open up. There are two main things to look out for on these items.

Hinges: If you have any type of item that has a lid on a hinge, you'll want to make sure that it has soft close hinges. This will prevent the lid from slamming down and catching little fingers. The hinges shouldn't be too tight, however, in the event that the baby manages to climb inside. The lid should be easy to push open from the inside.

Air Flow: If a baby or child were to get stuck inside, it's important that they can get air. If your storage piece doesn't have any holes or vents, drill some yourself. However, keep in mind that if you alter an item, you may void the warranty. It's also a good idea to check with a safety expert first.

baby gates & barriers

You won't need to worry about baby gates until your baby is mobile, but it's good to have an idea of what you'll be up against! Baby gates aren't the prettiest thing to look at, but they are very important, especially in a two-story home. You'll want to use a baby gate anywhere that there are accessible stairs, and in any other areas you want to keep the baby out of.

Baby gates can also be rearranged to keep the baby inside of a specific area, rather than to keep them out. Some parents will "wall in" a room that's been fully baby-proofed, like the nursery, or use a longer baby gate to create a playpen. Gates come in a lot of styles and designs, so you can look around for the ones that suit your home the best.

choking hazards

Babies like to put everything in their mouth, especially if they are teething. Our homes are filled with a surprising number of tiny things, and they all need to be kept out of baby's reach. Take some time to go through your home and find all those small items—things like paper clips, coins, buttons, etc.—and make sure they are safely stored. If you have another child in your home, you may also need to go through their toys.

fall or tipping safety

Whenever I'm installing a nursery, we always bring hardware to secure all the furniture to the walls. Things like dressers and bookcases can be hazards if a child tries to climb on them. Again, this isn't something you will need to worry about with an immobile newborn, but it's good to either get it all done early or know ahead of time what you'll need to do. Any furniture with drawers or shelves, or that could fall when weight is placed on it, should be attached to the wall.

earthquake & weather safety

Depending on where you live, you may also have some additional safety measures to consider. Do you live in a location that has earthquakes or tornados? If so, you might need to pay extra attention to certain things in the nursery. If there is any reason that things might move around (like in an earthquake), you'll want to take a few extra measures.

I work mostly in California, so I always bring earthquake putty with me to installs. I put it under items that could fall down, like decorative items on a floating shelf. It can also be used underneath the corners of picture frames to prevent them from moving on the wall.

Furniture quality also comes into play here. While it might be tempting to buy very inexpensive furniture for the nursery, consider that if it's low quality, it could fall apart if pulled on or climbed on (even if you've properly secured it to the wall). You'll want your furniture to be sturdy enough that if a child does try to climb on it, it won't buckle or break.

a final note

While we've gone over a ton of safety information, there very well could be even more depending on your specific circumstances, room layout, or furniture and décor choices. When in doubt, always do extra research! This applies to everything you buy for your baby, not just nursery items, and can even apply to your entire home. Ask family and friends, read online forums, and always read the fine print when shopping for any product.

Make sure to fully secure any furniture that can be climbed to the wall, like bookcases. Once baby is mobile, keep only soft items on the shelves.

CHAPTER 4

Budget

L et's talk numbers! Almost every time I take on a new client, one of the first questions they have is about budget. It's hard to set a budget if you don't know how much things cost, or how much you should allow for each item. Budgets come in all sizes, and you don't have to break the bank to get a beautiful nursery.

Left: Orchid Linen pattern designed by Holli Zollinger

determine your budget

When I start a new design project with a client, I always ask what their budget is. It seems like a no-brainer, but a surprising number of people respond simply with, "I don't know." That's not to say they have an unlimited amount to spend—even my most high-end projects have a budget—but it can be difficult to choose a number to stick to, especially during this transitionary time.

If you're like most people and unsure where to start, the first thing I recommend is to find your "scary number." When I do this with my clients, I start saying numbers, starting low, and ask them to tell me when I hit a number that makes them flinch. When I hit that number, I know that they are likely uncomfortable going above it. You can try this exercise yourself! Once you know your emotional upper limit, write that down and hold to it!

Also keep in mind that your budget can and may change. You might come across something that you just absolutely have to have and are willing to stretch the numbers. Alternatively, you could experience an unexpected drop in income and need to pull back on a few things. Having a general idea of how much you want to spend is a good idea, but also know that it's not set in stone. I've had clients change their budgets halfway through a project—it's not all that uncommon. We just sit down and evaluate where we are and what changes need to happen to get back on track.

Right: Don't worry if you don't have a crib yet. A bassinet or co-sleeper will work just fine for the first 3 to 4 months.

the essentials

As you think about your budget, it can be handy to know what you will absolutely need. If you are on a tight budget or are working with a small space, these are the must-haves:

A Place for Baby to Sleep: Babies sleep. A lot. You'll need a safe place for him or her to sleep that is separate from your bed. You can of course go with a crib, or just a bassinet or co-sleeper. Make sure you research all the safety elements, and keep in mind that babies can only stay in a bassinet or co-sleeper for three to five months.

A Place to Change the Baby: The good news is that you can change a baby pretty much anywhere. You can get a changing pad and put it on any surface, or even just a changing mat to use on the floor.

Somewhere to Store Baby's Things: You will need to figure out where to put the baby's clothes, toys, books, and diapers. They don't all have to be stored in the nursery, but they will need to go somewhere!

A Place to Feed and Rock the Baby: You will be doing a lot of feedings, especially when your baby is a newborn, so having a comfortable place to do that is important. If you don't want to purchase a glider or rocking chair, you can use your sofa or even your bed.

how much will it cost?

The short answer to this question is that nursery design costs can be almost anything—it depends on the size of your space, your specific needs, and, of course, your taste. However, there are certain general rules that will help you get a feel for what to expect. Design aside, this special space is about your baby, and you want your baby to be safe. If you're on a very tight budget, consider safety first , and refer back to that list of essentials on page 58.

furniture

Nursery furniture can vary drastically in price depending on the size, materials, and quality. At the very low end, a crib and changing table combination can cost around $300, while at the high end, a crib alone can be $3,500.

Consider Quality: Even the tightest budget should consider the safety of the baby, and furniture quality is one area where you may really think about investing. If you're going to buy a budget crib or a used one, go see it in person and make sure it's sturdy. Wiggle it, pull on it, and look for any weaknesses in the joints that may pose a problem down the road. Make sure you have access to the instructions and that no parts appear to be missing. In addition, you can visit www.CPSC.gov (Consumer Product Safety Commission) for current recall information. Baby products are recalled a lot more often than you might think, so I also recommend getting on the CPSC mailing list so you can be notified of any upcoming recalls. If possible, purchase a new and unused crib that's sturdy and from a brand that doesn't have past recalls (you can also look this up on the CPSC website).

Consider Longevity: Inexpensive furniture might not last very long, so think about how many years you plan to use it. If you want to keep the dresser until your child goes away to college, or are planning to use it for future children, you may want to invest in something of higher quality, or you'll likely have to replace it and spend more anyway down the road.

Consider Your Floor Plan: If you have a small space and can only fit a crib and changing table, you won't need to spend money on any other furniture. But if you have a large space you may want to consider other pieces, like a bookcase or armoire, and you'll have to build those into the budget. If you're feeling especially stuck or uncertain about your budget, I recommend that you do a floor plan before you finalize your budget. That way, you can see what you have room for. If you want to get started on that, you can jump to the Floor Plan chapter and refer back to this section when you're ready.

Right: My client owned these stunning custom-made curtains already, and we used other custom items in the room to make it feel luxurious.

window treatments

Window treatments are notoriously pricey and can be one of the biggest expenses in a nursery, especially if you have them custom made. You'll learn more about window treatments in the Textiles chapter, but they do serve a purpose and are important to have in the nursery to prevent unwanted light and UV rays in the room (which can cause problems for both safety and sleep patterns). As you consider window treatments, here are some questions to ask:

- How many windows do you have? If your space has a lot of windows, you may end up spending more money to cover them all, especially if you want the room to be blacked out.
- If you have oddly sized or shaped windows, things can get even trickier. It's not common to find ready-made window treatments for anything other than standard windows, so you may have to go the custom route if you want them done properly, and that can cost a pretty penny.
- Don't forget about hardware! While you may be able to find curtains at a good price, don't forget about the price of the curtain rod, brackets, and rings you might need. If you have multiple windows, this can add up quickly.

- You may also need help installing your window treatments. If you're not keen on DIY, factor in the cost of a professional to assist with hanging your curtain rods or roman shades. If you go with a company to custom make anything, make sure to ask how much installation costs or if it's included.

SAFETY FIRST

Refer back to the Nursery Safety chapter for tips on window treatment safety before you start shopping so you know what to look for and what to avoid

Left: Consider balancing budget items with custom pieces. When Jamie Baslow designed her nursery, she chose affordable furniture paired with a custom painting by artist Diane Rieger.

artwork & décor

Beautiful artwork and décor can be found even on a budget, especially with all of the options available online. If you like DIY projects, there are hundreds of nursery décor ideas out there. As you select art, the first question is to determine how *much* art you might want. Do you prefer the look of heavily decorated rooms, or spaces that are more simple? Consider the room you have and how much wall space is available. That will help you determine how many pieces you need and how much to budget for each one.

Artwork is often the most personal touch that goes into a nursery, so I do suggest putting some of your budget here to make the room feel personal and unique. If you find a piece that you really love and can see yourself loving for years to come, that might be a good place to splurge. It doesn't have to be a fancy original piece of art—it could even be something you make yourself.

Left: Design by Chaney Widmer of Mix & Match Design Company
Right: You can save a lot of money by doing things yourself. Keep a list of what you can and are willing to do!

installation

While you're shopping, pay close attention to what you need to install each item. There's nothing more disappointing than finding the right shelves, getting them home, and realizing that you don't own a drill to hang them with! Not all items will come with detailed directions, and some have parts that you'll need to purchase separately. A classic example is curtains: you might find the perfect fabric, but can you install the curtain rod yourself?

Painting the room, hanging wallpaper, installing a new ceiling fixture, etc., can all be very costly if you have to hire a painter, a wallpaper installer, or an electrician. For a budget-friendly nursery, choose items that don't need specialty installation or that you can handle yourself. Contracting pricing varies greatly depending on the service and your location. Call around for a few estimates early on so you'll know what types of items to shop for, or to avoid.

Like I've mentioned, I don't generally suggest buying a used crib since there could be safety issues, such as a drop-side or questionable quality. If you do inherit or are gifted a second-hand crib, make sure to thoroughly check it for structural integrity and safety—every tiny little part should be in place and secure. Check with the manufacturer to get a copy of the instructions, warranty, and product registration if possible.

some more budgeting tips

Once you have a sense of what you can or want to financially commit to the nursery, and how much everything costs, a few quick budgeting tricks can help you prioritize your spending, make sure you account for everything, and ensure you're making the most of your budget, no matter how big or small!

- Make an extra copy of the Nursery Checklist (pages 15–17) and use it to enter "guesstimates" for the items you've been considering. This will help you determine what you can afford, and which items you want to allocate the most budget to.
- Decide which items are the most important to you, or that you're willing to invest in. Then decide on a few items that you'd be willing to cut out should your budget get tight. This will help you figure out where to splurge and where to save.
- Don't forget about contracting! You might need to budget time or money to have someone paint the walls, install wallpaper, install a light fixture, etc. These costs can really accumulate, and the work typically gets done toward the end of the project once most of the budget is already spent.

- You may also be registering for some nursery items or receive them as gifts. Remember though, just because you register for something doesn't mean someone will purchase it. Make sure you can still afford everything you need.
- Always allow some wiggle room in your budget for shipping charges and deliveries, especially for large furniture items.
- Don't forget to include any sales tax you'll have to pay on your purchases.

Right: When I worked with Sierra Dallas Mallozzi on her nursery, we combined higher-end pieces with affordable ones to create a cohesive look.

buying secondhand

A great way to keep costs down in your nursery is to buy things used. Make sure anything you do buy is in good enough shape to be sturdy, safe, and secure. If you're looking into vintage items, be wary of lead paint that may have been used in past decades. Used and vintage pieces can be fantastic—you can purchase a vintage dresser and repaint it, or a used rocking chair that just needs a new cushion. Use your imagination and try to see the hidden potential. A quick upcycle might just get you the dresser or nursing chair you've always dreamed of.

money saving tips

Being a savvy shopper can make a big difference when you're trying to save money on any design project. Below are some tips for conserving where you can, and using your budget as effectively as possible.

- Shop around for prices online. If you find an item you like, search for the brand and product name on different websites to see who has the lowest price or free shipping. Be wary of any website that doesn't look legitimate or is one that you've never heard of. Many retailers also have price match guarantees—don't be afraid to speak up if you notice a competitor offering a lower price.

- Do some DIY. Things like painting the room or even installing wallpaper can be done yourself with a little research and watching some videos online. If you're totally new to DIY, start with smaller projects first. Installing wallpaper is definitely not easy!

- Wait for items to go on sale. This one can be a little risky because if you wait, you also run the risk of an item going out of stock, but many brands do run occasional sales that you can keep an eye out for.

- Lots of companies offer coupons or discounts if you sign up for their mailing list. These are usually prominently displayed on their website.

my budget:

$ _____

splurge on   save on

CHAPTER 5

The Floor Plan

Having a good nursery floor plan can make all the difference! Not only will it help you achieve a safe and functional space, but it will also give you an idea of what you need to shop for.

Left: Boho Flamingo Coastal pattern designed by Holli Zollinger

understanding your space

The nursery floor plan may seem like the least exciting part of nursery design, but it can also be the most important. This room needs to be functional, convenient, and safe. You don't want to end up in a situation where you *think* things will fit, and then they don't, or they do fit, but don't function properly. Use the information in this chapter, combined with what you learned in the Nursery Safety chapter, to create a floor plan that makes sense for your specific space.

The nursery is often the smallest room in the home—more often than not it's the room that was once the office or guest room. It may even be a large closet (which is where my first nursery was—my parents had a walk-in and put my bassinet in there). It may seem like there is plenty of space because a crib is so much smaller than a bed, but looks can be deceiving! Remember, for safety reasons cribs can't be placed just anywhere (see the Nursery Safety chapter), and you'll likely also want a changing table and glider as well. And that's not even including other storage like a bookcase, armoire, or toy box. The better (and sooner) you understand your floor plan, the easier things will be down the line. Avoiding mistakes up front is definitely better than trying to fix them later!

drawing your space

Before you dive in, you need to know what you're working with! Having a clear, accurate visual representation of your space will save you time and headache later. Above is a sample floor plan. Use the graph paper on the next page to draw out your space. Then you can add in furniture and see how things will fit.

When measuring doors and windows, measure from the *outside* of the casings. Also measure the space above and below the window frames. When measuring ceiling height, measure from the floor to the bottom of any crown molding, and again to the full ceiling height and make note of both measurements.

Be sure to account for all doors (including sliding doors for closets), windows, switches, and electrical outlets in the room.

If you're having trouble visualizing how the floor plan will translate into your actual space, try using some painter's tape or newspaper to lay out where you think the furniture should go.

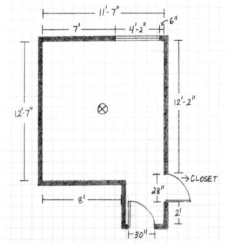

Ceiling height:

Space below window(s):

Size of any existing furniture that will stay:

Other Notes:

start with the essentials

The largest and most important pieces of furniture will be the trickiest to fit into your space, so I always suggest starting with those. Smaller pieces, such as wall shelves, lighting, and artwork, will be easier to move around.

the crib

You can't have a nursery without a crib, so start by figuring out where this most essential piece of furniture will go. A standard crib is approximately 56 inches wide and 32 inches deep, although it can vary, so if you're looking at a specific crib, get the exact measurements from the manufacturer. As you decide on placement, keep the following in mind:

- The crib should not be placed underneath a window or a mirror, since direct sunlight and/or breaking glass can be a safety hazard. For more crib safety information, see the Nursery Safety chapter.
- There shouldn't be any other furniture too close to the crib, where the baby can eventually use it as a stepping stool to get out of the crib.
- If you can, situate the crib so the baby can be seen from the entry door. This comes in handy if you put the baby down for a nap and leave the door open, so you can peek into the room without walking inside.
- The crib is also usually the focal point of the nursery, so it looks the best if it's on a wall with space around it that you see right when you walk into the room.

Left: Design by Allison Murray of @tailormadetudor
Right: It's best to have the crib on its own wall, as in this nursery designed by Elizabeth "Bitsie" Tulloch.

the glider/rocker

Next you should evaluate where your glider or rocking chair can go. Because of their motion, gliders and rocking chairs take up a lot more space than you might think. While you can find a variety of sizes, even the smallest ones are usually 30 inches wide, minimum. Because gliders often have a longer lead time as well, I like to consider their placement early on.

- The glider or rocking chair will typically go in a corner. Make sure you leave enough room so the chair can glide or rock forward and back, or swivel if it has that feature. You'll want enough space so the chair can fully extend backward without hitting the wall, and this can often be a pretty significant amount of space depending on the type of seating you get. Recliners may require even more space behind them.

- If you plan on using an ottoman, allow space for that too. If your room is small, I like to suggest choosing an ottoman that is lightweight and easily moved so you can put it in a corner when you're not using it, or when you want to use the open floor space for playtime.

- Leave space for a side table. Since you will likely be spending a lot of time in that chair, it's nice to have a small place to set something down, have a glass of water, or keep a small table lamp.

- You can also use a cozy chair that doesn't glide, recline, or rock, which will take up less room since you won't have to worry about leaving extra space behind it.

- Because gliders and rockers don't sit flat against the wall like a crib or dresser, they really can be tricky to find a spot for, especially if you have a small room or a lot of doors. If you just can't fit one in, you can always use a chair in another room or the sofa to feed and soothe the baby, then carefully transfer them into the nursery to sleep. You will likely be doing feedings in the middle of the night, so make sure that whatever spot you choose is easily accessible at night, and clear a path so you won't trip on anything.

Right: In Melissa Molinaro's nursery, we were able to put the glider in a little niche, giving it an extra cozy feel.

the changing table

You may be surprised that the dresser or changing table is third on this list since they take up so much space. The good news, though, is that dressers range greatly in size and are therefore easier to shop for in a specific size. They are also much easier to customize.

- A typical changing pad is about 32 inches wide, so if you're planning on using the dresser as a changing table, it will need to be wide enough to accommodate that.
- Ideally, you'll want to place the dresser on a wall with an outlet nearby to plug in things that may be sitting on the dresser, like a lamp, sound machine, or wipe warmer. It's best if the outlet is directly behind the dresser so you can hide all the cords (for both aesthetic and safety reasons).
- Depending on how the dresser is placed, you may need to also consider the space needed to open the drawers. Make sure you have enough space for the drawers to fully extend, and also enough room for you to stand in front of them while they are open.
- You will also need space on at least one side of the dresser for a diaper pail and/or trash can.

- Ideally, don't place the dresser or changing table below the window, as it can be used as a stepping stool and give your child access to the windows. If it does have to be placed under a window, add safety locks to the windows and the dresser drawers.

SAFETY FIRST

When you're working on the changing table area of your floor plan, keep in mind that everything you need to change or clothe the baby should be reachable. If you turn around or walk away from the changing table to get something, the baby can roll off. If your changing table doesn't have adequate storage, add some wall shelves or another storage unit nearby. Worst case, change the baby in another room, or on the floor.

Right: You can use any dresser to use as a changing table. In Jamie Baslow's nursery, she opted for a Mid-Century inspired dresser and added a changing pad on top.

other furniture

Now that you can see what space is left over, you can plan for remaining items, like an armoire, bookcase, or toy box.

- Consider additional pieces that allow for storage, like a toy chest, shelving, or a small bookcase.
- Corners and other awkward empty spots can be filled with storage baskets, a hamper, or even a large stuffed animal. These all take up floor space, though, so they should be included in a floor plan.
- Side tables come in lots of shapes and sizes, but round is usually the easiest to fit next to a glider (and also the safest).
- If you have the space, I like to suggest adding extra seating for a second adult in the nursery. I love storage benches for this since they have a dual function. Just make sure you read about storage safety in the Nursery Safety chapter.

area rugs

So many of my clients struggle with choosing the correct size area rug. Most often, I see people buying a nursery rug that is too small. A small rug that fits in between all the furniture may *seem* correct, but it will actually make your room look smaller. The ideal rug is one that's big enough to cover the center of the room and go underneath each major piece of furniture. A larger rug will open up the space, protect more of the flooring underneath, and give baby more space to crawl and play. It also helps make the floor look more expansive, which gives the room a more cohesive and pulled-together feel.

When measuring for a rug, take note of where your doors open into the room. If the rug pile is too thick, the door might not swing over it. Either choose a rug thin enough to slide under the door, or one that's smaller and doesn't overlap with the door swing. If you're up for a project, you could also opt to have your doors shaved down.

Left: Designed by Nikki Anderson

other décor

There may be some other décor items that will need to be considered in the layout. You may have items in addition to the ones below, but you can follow some of the same rules.

- **Artwork and Photographs:** Consider the walls as well. What size artwork will fit over the crib? What other wall space do you have?
- **Floating Shelves:** Adding some wall shelves can add a functional and decorative touch to your nursery. Since you may put things on the shelves that could fall down, it's important to never put wall shelves over a crib.
- **Floor Lamp:** Make sure to place a floor lamp in a place where a child can't tip it over once they are mobile. You may also want a lamp near the glider for nighttime reading or feeding.
- **Plants:** Plants are more and more popular in nursery design, but they can take up space, especially if you want a larger floor plant. Make sure you have the space for not only the pot, but the span of the plant itself (which can be wider than the pot). Always research the safety of any plant you put in the nursery—some are poisonous!

- **Window Treatments:** Believe it or not, window treatments may need to be considered in your floor plan. For example, if you're planning on installing curtains, each curtain panel should typically extend past the window frame by 6 to 10 inches on both sides, which takes up wall space and may affect the size of artwork or other wall décor. Same goes with roman shades—if you're putting anything on the windows that extends past the window frame, you'll need to take that into account when shopping for other wall décor.

Right: Consider keeping some floor space for playtime, even if it's just a small corner. Nursery by Ashley Joy Houston. Mural design by Betty Larkin.

space for play

When laying out your floor plan, think about where you plan on having your baby play. Some parents like the nursery to remain a serene place for only sleeping and nursing, while others want it to be a fun and playful multipurpose space. If you decide on incorporating a play area, make sure to account for any additional furniture you might want, like a play table, an easel, or beanbag reading chair, and for the storage of arts and crafts supplies and larger toys.

When Chaney Widmer of Mix & Match Design Company designed this small nursery, she opted to put a mini crib in the closet to save space.

small spaces

I've worked on hundreds of nurseries and so many of them are smaller rooms. Small spaces are definitely challenging, but there are plenty of ways to maximize the space, get creative, and design a space that's inviting, safe, and cozy. Here are some of my tips for working with a small space.

Take Advantage of Vertical Space: Put up some wall shelving. Book ledges in particular are great because they are shallow and don't stick out into the room. No room for a side table? Try a small wall shelf or even your windowsill if it's near the glider.

Expand Beyond the Nursery: If a full-size glider doesn't fit in the nursery, consider rocking the baby in another room of your home. If you don't have enough storage for toys, get a storage bench or some baskets to keep in the living room. You can even keep a bassinet, mini crib, or full-size crib in your bedroom.

Add a Mirror: One of my favorite tricks for a small nursery is to use mirrors. Hang a nice size wall mirror over your changing table—this will help reflect light around the room and make the space feel larger. Just be sure that the mirror is super secured to the wall, and never hang a mirror over a crib.

Keep it Light and Bright: Lighter colors help a space feel more open. Choose a light wall color and take advantage of any natural light, which will give your space a more open feel.

Be Mindful of Scale: If you have a small room, it may seem appropriate to get a small area rug and short curtains. The opposite is true! A larger area rug will help visually expand the floor, and hanging curtains high and wide will make your windows and ceiling height appear larger.

Say Goodbye to Clutter: Clutter makes a space feel smaller. Don't put anything in the nursery that doesn't need to be there, and keep the space organized. There will be a lot more organizational tips in the Organization & Storage chapter!

Get Creative: There are so many creative solutions for small spaces. Don't be afraid to think outside of the box!

- If you're tight on storage, consider putting a small dresser in the closet.
- If your closet doors open out into the room and block furniture, you might remove the doors and put up curtains instead.
- Use a C-table as a side table. This type of table is made so the base slides under the chair so it doesn't take up any floor space.
- If you don't have the space for a floor lamp near the glider, you can use a wall sconce. There are plug-in options available so you don't even need an electrician (just make sure you follow the cord safety rules from the Nursery Safety chapter).
- Mini cribs are a great option if you can't quite fit a full-size crib. In addition to being smaller, mini cribs also typically fit through doorways so they can double as portable cribs (most come with wheels).
- There are cribs available with storage drawers underneath. It's not a ton of storage, but definitely enough to store seasonal clothing or extra blankets.

awkward spaces

Sometimes the nursery isn't a perfectly square or rectangular room. Some homes have curved walls or angles, or doors and windows placed in strange spots. Above is the floor plan for a triangular shaped room I worked on—talk about a challenge! We needed to find a way to safely place the crib under the window because it was the only spot it would fit to allow all the other furniture. In order to solve the safety problems, we used full shutters (that would be kept closed) and solid blackout curtains to protect from heat and light; we also pulled the crib away from the window.

As always, you should take every precaution not to place a crib under a window. If you need to do it because of your layout, consult a professional baby-proofer to ensure you cover all the safety bases.

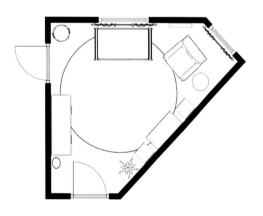

This nursery was a very odd shape, so we had to put the crib under the window. To make sure it was safe, the shutters remain fully closed, the window is always locked, the crib is pulled away from the wall, and full blackout curtains provide extra heat and light protection.

There wasn't any closet space in this nursery, so we added a clothing storage rack that fit the design of the room.

CHAPTER 6

Color & Theme

Choosing a color palette and potentially a theme for your nursery are the next big steps to getting your design underway! These don't need to be set in stone just yet, but it's a good idea to have something in mind so you can start shopping for décor.

color

One of the most popular articles I've written in my career was about how color affects your baby. The truth is, nobody *really* knows. This is why I suggest that you choose a color scheme that makes *you* happy. After all, you will be spending a lot of time in this space as well. Even if you don't want a colorful nursery, I urge you to read on.

The other issue that comes up a lot with color is the idea that girls should have pink and boys should have blue. While this is fine to do if you like those colors, you definitely don't have to stick to those norms. By the same token, if you're not finding out the sex of the baby, you don't have to strictly stick with yellow and green. I like to encourage an open mind and creativity here. If you're having a girl but you hate pink, don't use pink. If you're not finding out, but you love blue, go for it! Girls can love blue too. Get my drift?

You may already have a color palette in mind, especially if you've already chosen a "seed" item. If not, look back at your inspiration ideas and see if there's an image, piece of artwork, or rug that you really love, and then pull colors from that. I tell my clients not to be limited here—anything can be an inspiration item! Open up your closet, look around your home, or take a gander at some of your favorite online shops. Go with what speaks to you!

Coo Coo Ca Choo artwork by Kerri Rosenthal

color "rules"

Once you've decided on a general color scheme, use the rules below to apply the color palette to the space. And don't worry if you're still not sure which colors you want to use, you can always come back to this section later.

- As a general rule, choose two neutrals (white, ivory, gray, wood tones—yes, they count as neutrals), one main metallic (gold, silver, copper, rose gold), and two or three colors. For example, your two neutrals could be white and ivory. Your metallic could be gold, and two colors could be blush pink and sage green. While this isn't a hard-and-fast rule, it's a good place to start. If you want a more colorful space, just add more color. We'll get into how to balance them all in a few pages.

- You can mix neutrals. Mixing white, ivory, cream, and taupe in the same room is completely acceptable!

- You can also mix metallics. If you like both gold and silver, you can mix those as well. As long as they are balanced, they will work. If you love gold but your home has silver doorknobs, fret not!

- Lighting plays a big part in how colors look in a space. If you're looking at paint or wallpaper samples, make sure to bring them home and look at them in the actual room, during daylight and with artificial lighting. You'll be surprised how much they change!

- Warm colors tend to feel cozy, while cooler colors are more calming. Darker colors can make a room feel smaller and lighter colors help to open up a space.

- Color isn't just for the walls! You can incorporate your color scheme anywhere in the room, whether it's a bright green crib, a floral-patterned glider, or even a pink diaper pail.

- Keep in mind that clothes, toys, and baby utility items will play a part too. The whole feel of the room will change once you start adding in your baby shower gifts and start accumulating toys. These items will be on the floor and on the changing table, so you'll see them often. If you're so inclined, you can register for items that will fit in with your color scheme, and don't be afraid to tell your friends and family what your nursery colors are.

Left: In Irene Khan's nursery, the blush pink, gold, and gray tones are all balanced throughout the space.

color psychology

The Color Psychology class I took in design school was incredibly interesting and eye-opening. There is a lot of research about how colors evoke certain feelings. Have you ever noticed how fast-food restaurants typically have red and yellow logos? It's because those colors grab our attention and have been shown to make us feel hungrier. Marketing and advertising companies have poured a ton of money into figuring out how we respond to color so they can sell things to us more effectively. But for interior design, it's all about creating a space that makes you feel good. For some people, that could be an energetic and fun feeling, and for others it could be calm and serene. Your choice of color will help you create the atmosphere that you want.

When I'm choosing colors for my designs, I don't just choose the trendiest color of the moment. I want to know from my clients how they want to *feel* in their nursery. Oftentimes, that information alone gives me enough to go on. As you narrow down your color palette, instead of trying to choose colors from scratch, first try to envision the mood you want the space to have and choose colors that evoke that tone. For example:

High Energy: Black and white, or neutral, paired with a few bright colors will create high contrast. You can also play around with neon colors!

Calm and Serene: Use subtle cooler hues like blues and greens, paired with neutrals and wood tones. All neutrals work well here too.

Cheery and Vibrant: A combination of soft and bright (but not neon) colors will give you a happy vibe.

Soft and Casual: Neutrals, soft pastels, and "antique" finishes.

Unique and Thought-Provoking: Grays and mid-tone shades of green with pops of jewel-toned colors.

Rustic and Natural: Browns, dark grays, and earthy tones. You can also add in multiple wood tones and dark metals, like iron.

Fresh and Modern: White paired with another cooler neutral and a few pops of a mid-tone color.

Luxurious: White and ivory neutrals paired with a few subtle colors and metallic accents. Colors that are slightly desaturated also read as more sophisticated.

Earthy and Bohemian: Lots of textured neutrals with pops of multiple colors and multiple metallics, all balanced and mixing together.

Even with all of these color associations in mind, the most essential aspect to color psychology isn't research—it's each person's individual reaction to color. What does this mean for your nursery? Simple! Your energy is more important than the color on the walls. Choose colors that make *you* feel good. Babies will be exposed to every color in the rainbow throughout their lives and will eventually make their own associations.

Right: Love a certain color? You can try a monochromatic space. Just make sure to mix in different textures and materials.

how to balance color

So you've chosen your colors—now what? The practice of actually applying color to your space is all about balance. If you choose to paint the walls a brighter or bolder color, it will be prominent in the space, so make sure you choose a color you are comfortable looking at for a long time.

Whatever color you choose for the walls, you will want to use it somewhere else in the room as well, in at least two other spots. Balancing color is all about repetition around the room. For example, if you have a pop of an accent color on one side of the room, add it somewhere on the opposite side of the room to balance the space. This is a great time to leverage some of your other design elements, such as shape and texture, to bring that color to life. If one of your colors is royal blue, you could use a round royal blue throw pillow in a textured fabric, a rectangular piece of artwork with royal blue accents, and a crib sheet in a smooth cotton royal blue fabric. You'll have the color balanced throughout the room, and also a variety of object types and textures to add interest and dimension.

Remember neutrals are a color too. If you have chosen a wood-toned crib, make sure to include one or two other similar wood-toned items in the space, and balance them just as you would with color. If you have an existing fixture in the room in a metallic, like a ceiling fixture with a chrome base, try to incorporate a little silver around the room as well for a cohesive look.

theme

Nursery themes are one of those things that can be beautiful and sophisticated, or just plain overwhelming. A lot of my clients think that they need to have a nursery theme, or that the theme has to be something concrete, like "safari" or "under the sea." This is not the case! What I love about nursery themes is that they can be almost anything, and they don't even have to be something juvenile. If there's a specific theme you know you want, great! This section will help you understand how to implement it. If you're not sure, keep reading for some clarity. And remember, you don't need to have a theme at all!

While many parents-to-be are eager to rely on a theme as a way to guide their nursery design choices, knowing how to choose a theme and implement it well can be challenging. In this section, we'll review some tips on creating a themed nursery that's tasteful and versatile, and that will grow with your child.

Left: Peyton Baxter used an ocean wall mural and surfboard for her beach-themed nursery.

concrete theme ideas

- Safari Animals
- Nautical/Ocean
- Moon & Stars
- World Traveler
- Nature & Trees
- Floral
- Woodland Animals/Forest
- California Cactus

themes based on overall style

- Bohemian Eclectic
- Modern Bohemian
- Mid-Century Modern
- Rustic Natural
- Glamorous
- Traditional & Tailored
- Coastal
- Vintage

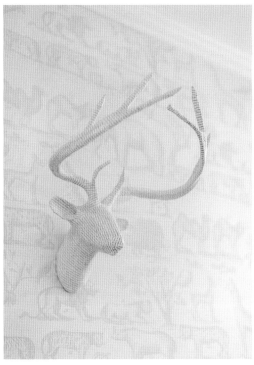

choosing a theme

Go with What You Like: Choose a theme that you like and can see yourself liking for many years. Don't choose a theme based on what's available or what you think your child will like—you're not psychic, and your child will develop their own preferences with time. The theme can be broad, like "animals" or it can be very specific, like "a day in Paris."

Get Abstract: A nursery theme doesn't have to be based on a sports team or television character. It can also be based on a concept, abstract idea, singular color, or even a feeling. For example, a nursery's theme could be "vintage," and it could be implemented by using patterns and colors that evoke a vintage feel.

Keep It Simple: Stick to thematic items that are smaller and inexpensive so you can trade them out later. Avoid thematic furniture or larger or expensive items. Down the line when your child starts to express individuality, they may request changes to their room. It's much easier to switch out some artwork and a pillow than a wall mural or furniture.

Commit: That said, if you really want a big thematic wall mural or some other large item that goes with your theme, be prepared to commit to it. Replacing items like these can be expensive and time-intensive.

Don't Worry about Matching: The nursery doesn't have to match the rest of your home (unless you happen to have a safari themed bedroom). Take this opportunity to have some fun and create a space that has some design elements that you've always dreamed of. Let your inner child play!

Ignore Theme Completely: A lot of my clients end up designing nurseries without a theme at all. I work with the feeling they want to get from the space to choose a color palette and pick décor pieces as we go without any particular theme in mind. While having a theme does make shopping easier because it narrows things down, a seed item can work just as well to guide your thinking and selections. If a theme decision is giving you stress, skip it! You can always add in thematic elements later if you change your mind.

This nursery doesn't have a specific theme, but still looks pulled together and cohesive. Designed by Jamie Baslow.

CHAPTER 7

Nursery Furniture

This section contains all you need to know about the right furniture to buy. Also, see the Nursery Safety chapter for more in-depth information about furniture safety.

the crib

The crib is the focal point of the nursery. It's a necessity to keep your baby safe, but it can be an anchor for the whole design. Because it's so central, it is also typically one of the first decisions I address when designing nurseries for my clients. It will be the centerpiece of the room, and it will help determine all of the other furniture used in the space. Cribs come in a range of shapes and sizes, and definitely vary in design, features, and quality.

Your child will not sleep in a crib forever, but a good quality crib means more than just a monetary investment—it means a better built piece of furniture, which is safer for your child. This is where your baby will spend a lot of time without you, and knowing that it's a solid piece that won't fall apart is worth a lot.

choosing a crib

When shopping for a crib, look for a furniture style that you love, but that also complements the style of your home. It's okay to stray a little out of bounds in the nursery if it means getting a piece that you'll like for the long term and that will grow with your child—these days, most cribs convert to a toddler bed, and some convert to a full-size bed. If you plan on having more children, you may consider choosing a neutral crib so you can reuse it in the future. When shopping for a crib, I suggest also purchasing the matching toddler rail at the same time, just in case that style is discontinued before you're ready to convert it. If it's in your budget, opt for white glove delivery (meaning the crib will be brought into your home and assembled for you). Assembling a crib is no simple task and requires two people, several hours, and usually a few swear words. If you assemble the crib yourself, make sure to do it inside the nursery! Most cribs will not fit through the door once assembled.

the mattress

Crib mattresses are highly regulated for health and safety, and there is no strict rule here. If you have a particular mattress in mind, you can do a little research to see if that brand has ever had a safety recall. Most crib mattresses are all standard size, but if you purchase a round, oval, or mini crib, those will have a specific mattress size that's different. Same goes for bassinets. In those cases, it's best to get the mattress from the same manufacturer to make sure it will fit properly and safely.

If it's in your budget, I always recommend going organic with the crib mattress. This surface will be close to your baby's face for many, many hours, and it's important to minimize the toxins your baby is breathing in. For more on toxins, see the Sustainable Nursery chapter.

PRO TIP

✔ Some cribs will be taller than others. Depending on your height, you might take that into consideration when shopping. You'll need to lean over the crib rail and into the crib to pick up the baby, so if you're on the petite side, you might want to get a crib that's lower to the ground.

---

the changing table

The only difference between a dresser and a changing table is that a changing table typically comes with a changing tray attachment on top that will hold your changing pad. A dresser will work just fine too, and changing trays are also available on their own so you can add one to any dresser. Dresser + changing pad = changing table. There are also some furniture pieces available that are specifically meant for a changing station only, but I generally don't recommend those because they aren't as versatile and you may end up having to buy a dresser down the line anyway.

The standard height for a changing table is around 34 inches, but if you're not average height, pay attention to the heights when shopping. Measure various surfaces in your home to see what height feels comfortable for you. Also keep in mind that adding a changing tray and pad on top will add a few inches.

A standard contoured changing pad is about 32 inches wide and 16 inches deep, but they can vary. There are also silicone changing pads that don't require a fabric cover and come in some additional shapes and sizes. Choose your changing pad first so you know what size changing table or dresser to look for. Also, if space and budget allow, opt for a dresser that's a bit wider so you have extra table top space for a diaper organizer, lamp, or a place to set things down while changing.

mattress height

Cribs usually come with two to four mattress heights. When you first assemble the crib, set it to the highest mattress height. Refer to the manufacturer's instructions for guidelines on when to lower the crib mattress. Make sure you keep the crib assembly instructions—you'll need them when it's time to lower the mattress.

hardware

Changing out the hardware on a dresser or changing table is one of the easiest ways to change the look of a piece without spending a lot of money. There are endless options out there for knobs, from pink crystal to starfish shaped. This is also a great fix for vintage pieces that need a little freshening up. All you need is a screwdriver!

Handles are trickier to replace than knobs. If you want to replace handles, measure the distance between the holes and shop for something that matches that measurement. There are a lot fewer options available for this though, so be prepared to do some digging. If your piece has both handles and knobs, it will be even harder to find a matching set.

drawer function

When shopping for a dresser or changing table, pay attention to the type of drawers it has. You will end up having to open and close them with one hand (the other on the baby), so you don't want a piece with drawers that are tricky to open or that may slam shut. This isn't an issue with good quality furniture brands since they usually have soft-close drawers, but if you're looking at lower end options or considering repurposing a regular dresser or vintage piece, make sure to check.

SAFETY FIRST

One thing to keep in mind when shopping for replacement knobs is that they aren't pointy or have sharp edges. Hardware should ideally be rounded—because of their placement, a baby can hit their head on them.

Left: We swapped out the knobs on this dresser for new acrylic-and-brass ones, giving the piece a whole new look.
Right: Penguin photography by Gray Malin

glider or rocking chair

The glider is another investment item that should be a good quality piece. You will spend a lot of time in the glider, so it should be comfortable and sturdy. There are a few types of nursery chairs available. The rocking chair, of course, is a perennial classic. Even though it poses some comfort issues, it has a beautiful look and is especially well suited to vintage inspired or traditional design styles. Gliders have a smooth gliding motion and usually look just like an upholstered chair. There are also wood frame gliders, which can be a bit less comfortable, but more affordable. Gliders can come with so many features nowadays, like phone charger plug-ins, electric recliner motors, etc., so if you're into tech, try searching out those options!

Whatever style you get, choose a fabric that can be easily cleaned. I cannot stress this enough! Some gliders are even available with slipcovers so they can be removed and washed in a washing machine (although they can be very difficult to put back on). If possible, go to a local store and try sitting in a few different styles to see what features you may like; you can also take a look at fabric samples in person. Many brands will ship fabric samples, which I also highly recommend looking into.

side tables

You might not think that a humble side table warrants its own section, but they can be an unexpectedly important piece in your nursery. You're going to need a place to put a baby bottle, a few books, your phone, and maybe even a small lamp while you're sitting in the glider. If you're able to fit a side table, I definitely recommend getting one.

If you do choose to have a side table, there are some specific things to look for and avoid. The main issue with side tables is that they are small and lightweight, meaning they can easily tip over. Because they are largely decorative, they can also have some design features that may be impractical or unsafe, such as sharp edges or wobbly legs.

I generally recommend that the top of the side table be round. Since side tables are lower than other furniture, sharp edges can pose more of a problem for curious children. The base of the side table should be sturdy on a variety of surfaces. Your side table may be placed on top of carpet or an area rug, which will destabilize it. It should be able to stand without wobbling and not be easily pushed down. Side tables with a stem or pedestal base are often not a great idea for this reason. As always, keep an eye on your baby's behavior and if they start trying to touch or pull on the side table, you may need to temporarily remove it from the room.

bookcases

If you have the space, adding in extra storage furniture is always a good idea. Bookcases are great because they provide vertical storage that typically doesn't stick out into the room, and they can also serve as display space for special items. When shopping for a bookcase, you'll want one that is at least 12 inches deep, since many baby books are large and bulky. You can also look for bins to go on the shelves to organize smaller toys and books.

Left: Design by Ashley Joy Houston
Right: Elizabeth "Bitsie" Tulloch chose a bookcase with a drawer to add even more storage to her nursery.

CHAPTER 8

Organization & Storage

S torage is a huge part of designing a functional nursery, and versatility is key. Babies and children come with a very unique set of storage needs, and if orga- nized well, your space will be able to accommodate the ever changing needs of a growing child.

identify your needs

Before you know exactly what furniture or organizational tools you'll need to keep things tidy and safely stowed away in the nursery, you'll first want to know the types of items you'll have to store. While the needs of every family—and thus, every nursery—are unique, the main items to consider are clothing, diapering supplies, and toys/books.

clothing

- A pile of infant onesies will rapidly give way to larger, longer pieces so be sure to have ample hanging space.

- If possible, organize your baby's clothing by size so you always have access to the correct sized item at any time. Their size will change quickly, so if you're organized, you can adjust to these changes easily.

- Drawer dividers are a great item to add inside your drawers to keep small items separated and organized.

- Purchase some baby hangers, since baby clothing won't fit on standard adult hangers. Again, I recommend hanging them in groups by size.

- Keep the "everyday" basics like onesies, pajamas, and extra socks in the dresser or changing table, since you will likely be getting your baby dressed or ready for bed right after a changing.

Right: A beautifully designed closet by Mackenzie Horan Beuttenmuller.

diapering

Changing a baby requires space for diapers, lotions, wipes, and ointments. You'll want these items close at hand to wherever you change your baby.

- Keep diapering items nearby and accessible. Consider a basket or organizer that sits on top of the changing table to keep diapers and other necessities close at hand. You can also use the top drawer of the dresser or changing table for diapers.
- You will also need some extra storage in the closet or nearby in your home for large packages of diapers. That way, if you run out, you don't need to leave the room while the baby is on the changing pad, which is a safety hazard.
- If you tend to change your baby in other rooms or areas of your home, you can get a diaper caddy to keep all the changing items in one place. Simply grab the caddy and bring it with you wherever you're going to be.
- If you have a two-story home or larger living space, you might even consider setting up a second changing station elsewhere in the home to avoid running up the stairs, especially for those all-too-common emergency blow-outs!
- As with clothing, you'll want to organize diapers by size, and always keep them refilled.
- Similarly, keep all the other diapering accessories (lotions, ointments, etc.) in one place and don't move them. The last thing you need is to stumble around trying to find something during a middle-of-the-night changing, or when you've got a mess on your hands.

toys & books

Toys are one of the most difficult things to store in a nursery because of their inconsistent sizes and shapes. You will also constantly be switching the toys they are currently using, and may often bring new ones in as well. Toys are unpredictable, so it's good to have lots of options for storing them.

- It's a good idea to have multiple places for toys. You might keep smaller toys in a drawer, medium toys in some bins or baskets, and larger toys in the closet (see more about closet storage later in this chapter).
- Wall shelves or a small bookcase are great for keeping books. If you like to display your books, book ledges are another great option. If you'd rather keep things clutter-free, you can neatly organize your books on a bookshelf, or keep them in the closet. I also like to suggest a "book box," basically a basket or bin that sits on the floor somewhere in the nursery where you can toss all the books each day.
- If you do purchase a toy box or storage bench with a lid, make sure it has safety hinges for slamming and suffocation protection (see more in the Nursery Safety chapter).

You can add drawer dividers to help organize your diapers and other changing items.

PRO TIP

✔ Don't forget the bathroom! Wherever you're planning on bathing the baby will need to have some storage as well. You'll need towels, baby hygiene and care products, a baby bathtub, medicine, etc. Make sure you have a dedicated spot for these items. You may need to add a small basket or bin to keep them organized and separated from your personal items.

Right: Designed by Jamie Baslow

textiles

Clean sheets, changing pad covers, receiving blankets, and burp cloths, to name a few, will all need a spot in the nursery. Keep the things you use the most close at hand, like in the changing table drawers. Heavier blankets or things you need less often can go in the closet.

- Crib sheets, changing pads, and stroller blankets are examples of textiles you may need to store. I suggest organizing these by type (burping pads, stroller blankets, crib sheets, etc.) so you can easily switch them out each time you do laundry.
- And speaking of laundry, you will need space for this too. Between the clothing, sheets, changing pad covers, and all the other things that you will need to wash (babies create a shocking amount of laundry!), you'll want a hamper or laundry basket somewhere in the room. Think about how far you need to treck to get to the laundry room and consider this when looking for a hamper. It should be easy to carry (often with one hand) and not too heavy.

get creative

Storage is often one of the biggest challenges in a nursery, especially since the nursery tends to be the smallest room in the home. Try to think out of the box to come up with ways to store things, like putting a dresser inside the closet, or getting an under-crib storage drawer.

If you find that you're out of floor space, go up the walls with your storage! If you don't want to take up floor space with a bookcase, use wall shelves instead. You can also put wall shelves higher up in a space to keep things that you don't need to access often. You can even put wall hooks on the back of your doors to hang a diaper bag, laundry bag, or towels.

SAFETY FIRST

I do not recommend using any storage unit that cannot be secured to the wall. If you choose something unique, such as a coat rack or small storage piece, be sure it is secured. See the Nursery Safety chapter for more information on securing items.

decorative storage

Just because it's holding a pack of diapers or a pile of hair bows doesn't mean that your storage can't also be stylish. Whatever you decide to use for storage can also be a design element in the space. There are lots of options out there for interesting and unique storage pieces, so don't feel like you have to stick with a standard bookshelf.

For example, consider using an upholstered storage bench, fun stackable cubbies, wall shelves in unique shapes, and patterned bins and boxes that can sit on shelves or go in cabinets. Storage and organization may seem boring, but I always like to consider it a design element and choose pieces that coordinate with the overall design of the room.

de-clutter

One of the biggest pieces of advice I can offer about nursery storage and organization is to declutter the space. If you have less stuff, you won't need as much storage and your organization will be more efficient. Depending on your personality, decluttering may be a hard sell. I personally love a good declutter session and use it for stress management, but I have plenty of friends and family who balk at the idea. If you're open to it, I suggest going through your whole home and getting rid of anything that you don't need or don't use anymore.

Decluttering the nursery is an on-going process. Because the items you and baby use will constantly change as they grow, you may need to declutter the space regularly. If you have other children, things may get shifted around between them as well. You can set a calendar alert for every six months and do your best to set aside a little time to go through old toys, clothes, and other things you may no longer want or need. A clean and organized nursery not only looks great, but it poses fewer safety risks and may even give you some extra peace of mind.

hang it up

You may find that you have a few items (such as a diaper bag, hooded towel, or saddle blanket) that you use frequently so you don't want to store it. Things like this can be kept on wall hooks. I love wall hooks because they are both decorative and functional. I suggest putting a few wall hooks near the entry door of the room so you can quickly hang items up as you walk in or out.

Right: Wall ledges are a great way to store books if you're short on space.

Humphrey
The Lost Whale
A True Story

story by Wendy Tokuda and Richard Hall
Illustrations by Hanako Wakiyama

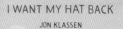
I WANT MY HAT BACK
JON KLASSEN

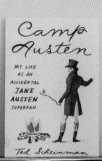
Camp
Austen

MY LIFE
AS AN
ACCIDENTAL
JANE
AUSTEN
SUPERFAN

Ted Scheinman

KNUFFLE BUNNY
A CAUTIONARY TALE BY Mo Willems

Du Iz Tak?

Carson Ellis

CHAPTER 9

Art, Décor & Walls

L et the fun begin! Now that the main furniture pieces are decided and you hopefully have a general color scheme or theme in mind, we can really focus on adding personality to the space and bringing it all together with artwork, décor items, and paint and/or wallpaper.

Left: Nude Roses wall mural by Rebel Walls

wall treatments

When I was a baby, my parents kept me in a bassinet in their bedroom. I was then moved into the nursery, which had been adorned with pastel floral wallpaper on all four walls. Of course I don't remember how I felt about it as a baby, but I remember it so fondly as an adult. It was the 80s and a bit tacky, but my parents chose it for me and that made it special. I have this image of my mom flipping through wallpaper books until she got to a pattern that made her smile. Don't get me wrong, I definitely begged my parents to let me change it as I grew older, even requesting to paint the whole room black sometime in my teens—a request I'm glad they denied! My point is, no matter what you choose for your nursery, no matter how simple or extravagant, it's a space for *you*. And you should paint or wallpaper it accordingly!

wallpaper

I've included the section on wallpaper first, even before paint, because if you're going to use wallpaper, it's a good idea to choose your pattern early on. The pattern or colors will make a real statement and feature of the room, so you'll want to choose colors, artwork, and décor that coordinates with it.

That said, I *love* wallpaper. It's a great way to add serious style in a nursery. There are so many patterns available now, including temporary peel-off styles that won't damage your walls. If you don't want to commit to covering the entire nursery, you can use it to bring pattern and variety to an accent wall, or even the ceiling.

All wallpaper is not created equal, so be careful with wallpaper calculators you may find online. The best ways to accurately determine how much wallpaper you will need are to consult an installer or call the manufacturer directly with your wall measurements. If you order too much, you will overpay, but if you order too little, you may not be able to find more stock in the same dye lot. I always recommend using a professional wallpaper installer since wallpaper can be tricky and expensive.

PRO TIP

✔ Don't forget the ceiling! The ceiling is a great place for a contrast paint color, ceiling medallion, or even a mural.

murals

As with wallpaper, if you want to do a painted wall mural, you'll want to decide on this a little early on. However, since wall murals are custom, it's easier to adjust colors. Having a mural painted is like using your walls as a canvas for one giant art piece! Murals can certainly be an investment, so make sure you work with your local muralist to come up with a design you really love.

Also, murals are best for those who are planning on staying in their home for years to come. If you're planning on moving soon, a mural might not be the right choice. Because they are often completely custom designed and usually quite personal, it can be emotionally difficult to paint over if you are moving or changing the design down the line.

Mural by Chelsea McGraw

wall decals

If you like the idea of wallpaper or a mural but don't want the investment, wall decals can be a great option. Wall decals come in almost any design and color, so the options are endless. They peel and stick right onto your walls and are completely removable. When installing decals, make sure you really press them on. They stick best to newly painted walls that are clean and dry.

wall texture & humidity

Wall texture and humidity are two things that can cause potential problems for wallpaper (especially removable wallpaper) and wall decals. If you have textured walls, often referred to as "orange peel" texture, or any other medium or heavy texture, wallpaper and decals may not adhere as well. If you want to go with traditional wallpaper that uses paste, there are special preparation measures that your installer can take, but these options are not available for removable wallpaper. Always order a sample and make sure it will stick to your walls!

Additionally, if you live in a home near the ocean, or anywhere that causes the inside of your home to be fairly humid, removable wallpaper and decals may have a harder time sticking to the walls.

paint

Painting the nursery can seem daunting, but it doesn't have to be. Here are some tips to achieve an easy and seamless transition to a new wall color. Keep in mind that paint is relatively easy to fix or change, so it's not as much of a commitment as wallpaper.

That said, beware of "empty room syndrome" after you've painted! I once had a client whose entire home was painted white, but she wanted more color in the nursery. We chose a soft pale pink to go on all four walls. As soon as the paint was done, she got concerned, feeling worried that it was *too* pink. That's "empty room syndrome." When you look at a room with nothing but pink, the only thing you're going to see is, well, *pink!* We hadn't yet added the white furniture, darker glider, curtains, rug, artwork, and all the other elements of the design to balance out the color. Once everything was in place, the pink receded to the background and looked great.

- When painting the room, it can also be a good time to freshen up the baseboards, casings, and other moldings if they need it. Moldings can even be painted a contrast color to become part of the design scheme.
- Paint comes in multiple finishes, such as flat, eggshell, satin, and semigloss. Flat paint has the least sheen and is also the hardest to clean. For a nursery, consider going with an eggshell or satin. If you're painting an attached bathroom as well, go for a semigloss to help repel water.
- Always choose a low or zero VOC paint (VOC stands for Volatile Organic Compounds, or toxic chemicals that are released into the air). Almost all major paint brands have low VOC formulas now, so they're easy to find, but head over to the Sustainable Nursery chapter for more information on chemicals. Even if you're using a low VOC paint, try to paint the nursery as early as you can to let any extra fumes dissipate. Keep windows open as long as possible after the paint is applied.
- Keep any extra paint. There may be some little dings to touch up once all the furniture is moved in. After the nursery is complete, store the extra paint in case you need it down the line for more touch-ups. If you don't have any paint left to store, make sure to write down the brand and color in case you need to buy more.

Left: A wall mural is a great way to get a customized look. Mural by Wall Art by Allyson.
Right: You can choose to paint an accent wall instead of the whole room.

decorative paint

If you want something more than just solid colored walls, but don't want to commit to a full wall mural, consider doing a decorative paint treatment. Either draw or tape out your design first, or hire a professional painter.

Geometric Shapes: You can use paint to create stripes, circles, or other geometric designs on the wall. You can do this as an accent wall as well—it works great on the crib wall because you can forgo hanging any artwork above the crib.

Ceiling Accent: Paint the walls a single color and the ceiling a different color. I recommend this particularly for rooms that have higher ceilings and good natural lighting. If your room is small and dark, a painted ceiling can make the room feel more closed-in.

Molding Accent: Paint the moldings of the room an accent color to highlight the architecture of the space. This is a bolder move, but it can look really amazing!

Ombre: You can paint the walls so they fade from one color to another. This is tricky, so if you decide on this effect you may want to hire a professional.

Monochrome: You can paint all the walls and molding the same color. This can give the room a very sophisticated look and it cuts down on contrast, which can make the space feel more serene.

Play Around! The best thing about paint? You can always paint over it.

Paint doesn't have to just be a solid color. You can paint stripes and geometric shapes as well—use your imagination! Nursery by Ashley Joy Houston. Mural design by Betty Larkin.

HOW MUCH PAINT TO BUY

✔ In general, a gallon of paint will cover about 300 to 350 square feet. To calculate the square footage of your walls, measure the width and height of each wall (in feet) and add them together. For example, for a room where each wall is 10 feet wide and 8 feet high, multiply 10 X 8 to get 80, then multiply by 4 (since you have four walls). That totals 320 square feet. You will likely need to paint two coats (potentially more if you're painting over a darker color), so you'll need to double the square footage to account for the second coat. Some paint calculators also subtract for windows and doors, but I like to round up so you have some extra paint for touch-ups or mistakes. Seal the leftover paint and store it safely with the color and finish labeled.

artwork & décor

You've hopefully purchased all your nursery furniture—a fabulous crib, functional changing table, cozy glider, etc.—and now you're staring at a room full of beautiful pieces with absolutely nothing on the walls. What should you do now? Have some fun! Your art and décor choices will likely be changed out in a few years, so you can really let loose in this area. But keep in mind that these items may not be kept forever. This is also a great opportunity for bargain shopping, vintage items, family heirlooms, or DIY projects.

Keep It Simple: There are two main types of nursery art out there—stretched canvases and framed prints. Decide which of these you prefer and look for nursery art in that material (or you can combine both).

- Canvases are great because they have texture and a "real" art feel. The other advantage is that they are lightweight and safe to hang over a crib (although anything hung over a crib should be properly secured as noted in the Nursery Safety chapter).
- Art prints on paper are very affordable, but you will likely have to frame them, which can add to the cost and the weight. I always recommend framing with acrylic instead of real glass in a nursery or kid's room.

My client Sierra Dallas wanted a personalized wall name for her daughter Capri, so we chose a mirrored rose gold piece to accent the other metallics in the room.

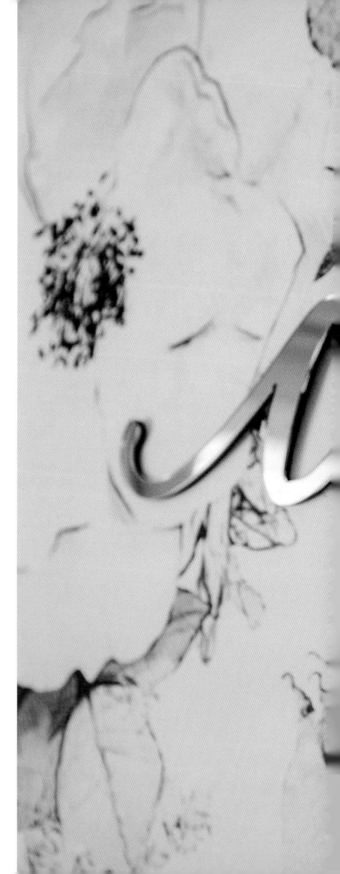

Add Flair with Framing: As mentioned above, you can frame an art print, but you can also frame a canvas, or pretty much anything you want.

- An unframed canvas has a modern appeal, but framing a canvas in an ornate frame gives it a whole different aesthetic. Look for vintage or painted frames at thrift sales or vintage shops.
- Framing adds weight and will change the overall size of the piece, so factor those both in to your decision.

Think Outside the Rectangle: Most art comes in a rectangular or square shape, but there are also other, more unique options. For example, you can purchase an unfinished wood wall shape and then paint it in colors that match the rest of your design. You could also choose a woven wall hanging or other more sculptural wall art.

Get Personal: There are a lot of great ways to personalize artwork for a nursery, whether it's getting the baby's name printed on an art canvas, using custom wall letters, or having a picture frame engraved. These touches are truly personal, and they can really give added warmth to your nursery.

- Wall names come in all shapes and sizes—wood, fabric, and even hand painted. You could also go with something even more dramatic, like a larger wood wall monogram, or a laser-cut design mounted on a wood background. I've even seen personalized hanging surfboards.
- Lots of art companies and websites like Etsy allow for customization—it can't hurt to ask!

Include Memories: Sometimes the best artwork in a nursery is something sentimental. Using old family photographs, a blanket hand-knitted by Grandma, or even a framed photo of your honeymoon are all great ways to keep memories alive in your space.

BUDGET SAVVY

$ If you're really on a tight budget for art, you can purchase downloadable art prints online and print them yourself at home. I've seen these prints at places like Etsy in the $5-8 range.

Left: Even books can be decorative. Get some fun bookends and choose your favorite books to display.

mirrors

I am a huge fan of using a wall mirror in the nursery. Adding a mirror will help to open up the space, bounce light around, and give you the opportunity to do a quick shirt-stain check. The natural spot for a wall mirror is over the dresser or changing table. If your floor plan is tricky and you can't put a mirror there (if your dresser ends up under the window), then you can add a smaller decorative mirror elsewhere on the wall. Mirrors are heavy and contain glass, so they need to be very well secured to the wall. Never put a mirror over the crib!

Mirrors are also the perfect item to use to incorporate your chosen metallic or wood tone. I've used countless gold mirrors over the years, and they never fail to add just the right touch! I also like to use round mirrors since they don't have any sharp edges and can help to soften the look of a room with a lot of other square and rectangular furniture (like cribs and dressers).

how to hang artwork
& wall decor

You will likely end up with artwork in many sizes for different spots in the room. It is always my advice to hang pieces along the same horizontal line, so either the top or center of each piece is the same height. I also suggest hanging artwork at eye-level, so the center of the piece should be about 5 feet, 5 inches from the ground. Of course, if you have very high ceilings, you may have to adjust. And remember, anything that gets hung over a crib should be heavily secured to the wall and should not have any glass (framed photos, mirrors, etc.).

area rugs

Most of the time, my clients will keep the existing flooring in their home and add an area rug in the nursery, even on top of carpet. Area rugs are a great way to add color and texture, and they also help to protect the flooring underneath. Needless to say, rugs also help protect your baby from falls and tumbles better than hard surfaces. Rugs come in all types of materials, but for a nursery, I suggest looking for cotton or a cotton blend. As you look for an area rug, there are a few things to keep in mind:

- Area rugs are notorious for looking different in person than they do online or in a catalog, so make sure there is a good return policy if you're ordering a rug without seeing it in person first.

- Avoid white rugs and pay close attention to how the rug should be cleaned. If you're worried about dirt showing, patterned rugs with multiple colors are best.

- Pay attention to the fiber content of the rug, especially if you have wool, latex, or other fiber allergies. Wool rugs are also known to shed or be itchy, while viscose rugs are beautiful and soft but don't hold up as well and are harder to clean. Cotton rugs are great for nurseries, but come in limited styles and colors. Polyester blends are usually soft and easy to clean, but can sometimes smell more than other types of rugs. We'll address smells from chemicals and toxins in the Sustainable Nursery chapter.

- Especially if you have hardwood floors, don't forget to purchase a rug pad! You'll be spending significant time on the floor with your little one, and your knees will thank you!

accessories

Accessories such as picture frames, decorative figurines, and other small décor items are often the last thing to add to a nursery, but they sure can affect the overall design! Choose pieces that make you feel happy and don't worry too much if they don't fit with the design. Accessories are generally small and can be moved around and changed often. Check out the Finishing Touches chapter for more on accessories and how to style them.

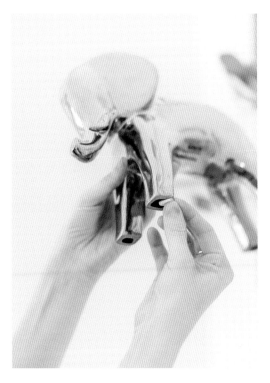

a safe shelfie

If you have a bookcase or shelving with accessories on it, purchase some earthquake putty (sometimes called museum putty) to stick under all the objects so they will stay in place. Earthquake putty is not permanent and is easy to remove, but it will help prevent your items from shifting or falling down in an earthquake, or just if the shelf gets bumped. You can also stick it behind picture frames so they don't tilt on the wall (a major pet peeve of mine!).

Left: In Jessi Malay's nursery, we chose accessories that accented her floral wallpaper in similar colors and patterns.

lighting

Lighting is one of the most important design elements in a nursery. It helps set the mood and can contribute to the overall function of the space as well as how the baby sleeps. I'm sure you've heard that light attracts bugs, right? Well, the same goes for humans. In fact, architects often use specially placed lighting to guide a person through a building without them even knowing it.

light fixtures

Like color, the type and amount of lighting in a room can also change the feel of the space. In a nursery, make sure you have multiple types of lighting, both for function and for comfort. Sometimes you'll want the room to be dim so you can rock the baby to sleep but still have enough light to move around safely. Other times, you'll need it as dark as possible to aid in baby's sleep. Assuming you also use the nursery to play and learn, an option for bright and open lighting can be important too. Flexibility is key.

Ceiling Fixtures: This is one area where you can really make a design statement. Since a ceiling fixture is totally out of reach of the child, it can really be anything you want it to be—sparkling crystal, a modern sputnik, or just a simple drum shade.

Well-Placed Lamps: Lighting in the nursery is the key to making the space function properly. Good overhead lighting (recessed lights, ceiling fixtures, etc.) is excellent for overall light in the room, but the ability to switch on

a table lamp near the changing table or glider is hugely beneficial for those late night visits to the nursery. Don't forget light bulbs with low to moderate wattage for soft light that's not too harsh.

Night-lights: Ever stubbed your toe in the middle of the night? Enough said! Beautiful night-lights are readily available, so find some you love and place them both in the nursery and also in any walkways/hallways leading to the nursery.

Dimmers: Dimmer switches allow you the maximum amount of flexibility, so if you're doing any electrical work, consider adding dimmer switches too. Make sure to check the type of light bulb, as some are not compatible with dimmers.

how to measure for lighting

Ceiling Fixture Width: As a general rule, take the width and length of your room, add them together, and then use the final number in inches. For example, if your nursery is 10 feet X 12 feet, add 10 + 12 to get 22. You should look for a light fixture that is a maximum of 22 inches in diameter.

Ceiling Fixture Height: The height of a fixture depends on two things: the height of your ceilings and the height of any people who may be spending time in the room. In general, the lowest point of the light fixture should be at least 7 feet off the floor. However, if someone

Bottom: A floor lamp can be tucked behind a glider for extra lighting. Just make sure cords are secure and it's not at risk of getting knocked over. Design by Abby Culora of Culora Me Green.

in your family is 6 feet, 4 inches, you might feel more comfortable with extra clearance. When calculating the height of a fixture, also keep in mind that you may have a few inches of chain at the top as well. If you have low ceilings, you can look for flush mount fixtures that are usually installed close to the ceiling.

Ceiling Fan Size: Ceiling fans are typically wider than most ceiling fixtures. To choose the correct size, calculate the square footage of your room and bring that with you when you're looking at ceiling fans. Each specific model should have a manufacturer's note about the size of room it is most appropriate for, taking airflow into account as well.

Table Lamp Size: If you're planning on putting a table lamp on a side table by your glider, there are a few things to consider. The table lamp should be smaller than the table. For example, if your side table is 18 inches in diameter, you'll want a table lamp that is several inches less than 18 inches in diameter (including the shade). Same goes for the height. However, if you have very high ceilings or larger furniture pieces, you can get away with a bigger lamp.

LAMP SAFETY

Table lamps really add to the design of a space, but in a nursery, there are a few quick safety tips I'd like to share. For more, see the Nursery Safety chapter.

- Pay attention to the base of the lamp. It should be heavy and wide enough that it won't tip over easily.
- Consider the material of the lamp (i.e., glass, ceramic, plastic, wood, etc.). A glass lamp is more likely to break if it falls or is pulled off the table.
- Keep any electrical cords out of reach so they can't be yanked on to pull the lamp down.
- Consider choosing a ceiling fan with a light instead of a chandelier or pendant—airflow is proven to help drop the risk of SIDS.

look up!

If you happen to have a high ceiling, you can take advantage of this feature by choosing a light fixture that has a long chain. When you're shopping, look for the minimum and maximum chain length to see if the fixture will work in your space.

CHAPTER 10

Textiles

T here are a lot of textiles that go into a nursery design—everything from crib bedding and window treatments to throw blankets, pillows, and sheets. It can be a lot to coordinate, and I'm here to help you work through it all.

Artwork over crib by Takashi Murakami

crib bedding

Choosing crib bedding can be one of the most fun parts of a nursery, but also one of the most confusing. You may notice that photos you see online or in catalogs show lots of different types of bedding—sheets, skirts, bumpers, bows, etc. This chapter will help you navigate what you need, what's safe, and what's stylish.

One note before you hop into this chapter—just because you see it in a photo, doesn't mean it's safe! Even in this book, you'll notice some images of hanging blankets, or pillows placed inside the crib. Sometimes the child who sleeps in that crib may be older, sometimes it's just photo styling, but *always* do your safety research when it comes to crib bedding. I cannot stress this enough. Most experts recommend never putting anything in the crib (even blankets) when the baby is a newborn.

crib bedding tips

The good news is that, by and large, crib bedding is all made to a standard size, so you won't need to worry about it unless you're buying a round, oval, or mini crib. If you do have a unique crib shape, you may want to consider custom bedding since there will be a lot fewer choices available.

Start with Samples: With fabrics, it's important to not only see what they look like, but also how they feel. If you're looking into a few styles of crib bedding, ask for fabric samples first. Samples will also help you coordinate with the other textile items you will need.

Sheets: The fitted crib sheet is the only piece of crib bedding that you really need. Purchase at least three to four fitted crib sheets, as you will need to change them frequently. You can even get multiple colors or patterns to change up the look. I like to recommend looking for organic crib sheets, especially since there are so many options available now.

Mattress Protector: In addition to a crib sheet, you can also get a mattress protector to go underneath, just like you would for a regular bed. For a nursery, I recommend one that is waterproof to protect your mattress from all of the things that can come out of a baby!

Skirts: There are a variety of styles available for crib skirts. However, skirt lengths may be different depending on the brand. When your crib is assembled with the mattress at the highest setting, measure from the bottom of the mattress to the floor to see what length your skirt should be. The catch here is that when you drop your mattress, the skirt will also get longer and may lay on the floor. Some people choose to remove the skirt at this point, or you can just push the extra fabric under the mattress and adjust it until it looks straight (the weight of the mattress should hold the skirt in place).

Bumpers: Crib bumpers are controversial and there are even a few states in the United States where they are banned. I always recommend skipping the bumper. There are options for alternative style bumpers that are less of a safety risk, like mesh fabric bumpers or braided material that allow for more airflow. You can look for these options online by searching for "breathable crib bumpers."

PRO TIP

✔ Not every crib will allow for a skirt. Some crib designs have hardware that gets in the way and a skirt can't properly hang down. I've found this to be the case more often with modern style cribs. If you're not sure, you can always ask the manufacturer.

window treatments

Window treatments can be beautiful, but in a nursery they also serve a very important function—to control light and heat. Some parents want to have the room completely dark, while some want to train their baby to sleep with some daylight. Others like to have both options. Take some time to think about what you might want for your baby—this might include a little sleep training research before you buy window treatments. Once you know your goals, here are some tips on choosing the best window treatments for your space.

Work with What You Have: Does your home already have blinds, shutters, or roll down shades? You don't necessarily need to tear them out! You can always add curtains over your existing treatments. If you already have curtains, you can keep the hardware and just update the curtains themselves. Alternately, you can keep the curtains and add a pull-down blackout shade underneath. Also, make sure to adjust any existing window treatments in accordance with the safety standards in the Nursery Safety chapter.

Curtain rings can be added to most readymade curtain panels.

curtains

Curtain Length: Curtains are typically hung so that they sit just about a quarter inch off the floor. However, you may opt to "puddle" the curtains for a more dramatic look. Add 2 to 4 inches to the total length for a soft puddle, or 6 to 8 inches for even more drama. If you want to go with puddled curtains, keep in mind that they will get dirtier than normal since they drag on the ground.

Curtains look best when they are hung high—just about 2 to 3 inches from the ceiling. This makes for a much grander look, adds height to the space, and helps block more light when the curtains are closed. To find your ideal length, I suggest measuring from the floor to the ceiling, subtracting 3" and then adding any extra length for a puddle if you want one. You may need to adjust the length depending on the type of hardware you purchase as well (see below).

Curtain Lining: You can find everything from sheer curtains to full blackout curtains. If possible, choose something with at least a UV protective lining to minimize heat transfer and reduce the risk of SIDS. If you like the look of breezy sheer curtains, layer them on top of roman shades or roller shades that have heat and light protection. You can even choose a double curtain rod and do two layers of curtains so you have both options.

Don't Forget Hardware: You will need a curtain rod, brackets, finials, and possibly rings. When you hang curtains, they should ideally overlap the outside of your window on each side by about 6 to 8 inches. Choose a curtain rod that is about 12 to 16 inches longer than your window (including the frame) to account for that overlap. You can find inexpensive adjustable rods at most bigger retailers. Your window hardware should generally match one of your chosen neutral colors, wood tones, or metallics.

Always Go Cordless: If you're installing roman shades, blinds, or any type of window treatment that typically has a cord, try to find a cordless option. For a detailed look at window treatment cord safety, see the Nursery Safety chapter.

Customize: There are so many options available now and many companies are offering customizable options for curtains and window treatments that are relatively affordable. Customizing doesn't need to mean expensive. It can be as simple as purchasing some ready-made curtains and then having them hemmed to the proper length at your regular tailor.

PRO TIP

✔ I always like to suggest adding curtain rings for nurseries since it makes it easier to pull heavier blackout curtains open and closed. If you opt for rings, you may need to adjust the overall length of the curtains since rings add about 2 inches to your hardware (your curtains will hang lower from the rod itself).

roman shades & roller shades

Romans are a very popular choice for nurseries as well because they have a clean and tailored look. The issue that I've run into with both Romans and roller shades is that they allow for light-leak around the edges, so if you're going for full blackout, it might be a challenge. Curtains will allow some light-leak as well, but most window shades are custom made so it's a much bigger investment to then have something that doesn't work for you. You can get ready-made Roman shades or rollers online, but in my experience it's hard to find them in exactly the right size for your window without customizing.

The other problem with Romans is that they often have a cord. There are cordless options available, but they won't work for every window (it depends on the type of window casing you have and the type of mounting system each company uses). Cordless roller shades are usually easier to find.

If you want to install any type of shade on your windows, whether it's a Roman shade, blackout roller shade, or any other shade, I highly recommend finding a local company that can come out and look at them with you, measure, and give you an estimate. That way you can communicate your needs and preferences to them and decide if it's worth the cost. A lot of companies will do free consultations.

changing pad covers

Changing pad covers come in a wide variety of fabrics and colors, but perhaps the most important thing is to choose a soft fabric since your baby's bare skin will be touching it multiple times a day. I also recommend that you buy in bulk. Because of the nature of changing pad covers, they are going to get dirty frequently, so I always recommend that you purchase at least three to four of them. If you've opted for a silicone changing mat, you won't need fabric covers.

pillows

Glider Pillow: The most important pillow in the nursery will likely be the glider pillow. Since you will be spending a lot of time in the glider (reading, nursing, rocking, etc.), you will want a pillow that provides good back support, like a lumbar pillow.

Throw Pillows: You can have a lot of fun with throw pillows (as long as they are kept out of the crib!). If you have a window seat or other area where you may want to incorporate some pillows, go for a variety of shapes and sizes. This is a great place to play with color and pattern, and add a pop of your accent color of choice.

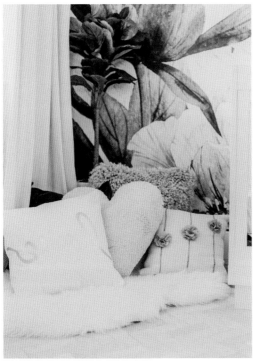

Bottom: Jessi Malay wanted a cozy corner to read and play with her daughter, so we added some floor pillows and a soft rug.

accent items

While you're shopping for your textiles, keep in mind that you may also want some coordinating upholstery in the space, like a window seat cushion or toy box cushion. Cushions are fairly inexpensive to have made (or make yourself) and can add comfort and warmth to the space. It's also a creative way to turn a flat surface into guest seating for others who may be spending time in the nursery.

Pillows should *never* be placed in the crib with a baby, and newborns should not be left around pillows unsupervised as they pose a suffocation risk. You may see pillows in the crib in nursery photos (including some in this book), but that is only for styling. See the Nursery Safety chapter for more information on crib bedding safety.

blankets

Blankets, as well as pillows, should be kept out of baby's crib, but you will definitely want to get a cozy blanket for the glider. You will be in and out of the nursery at all times of the day and night, and having a soft blanket for yourself will come in very handy. Look for soft fabrics that are machine washable, and make sure the blanket is large enough to cover you.

Left: If your nursery has a window seat, you can add a cushion and/or pillows to pull the whole design together.
Right: Designed by Nikki Anderson

CHAPTER 11

Installation & Contracting

S o you've purchased all your furniture, décor, and artwork, but now you need to get everything actually installed and completed in your nursery. Here are some tips on how to get your nursery in place, from deliveries to DIY to dealing with hiring contractors.

get it together

Installing your nursery can be very simple or very complex depending on the items you've chosen and how much contracting will be involved. For those of you who love a good DIY project, this is your time to shine!

One piece of advice I'd like to share before you get started on your installation is to stay realistic about the timing. Even things that sound simple, like putting together the crib, can often turn out to be difficult and stressful. I've seen cribs come together in thirty minutes, and others take hours. Give yourself ample time to plan out each project in the nursery so you can enjoy the process!

shipping & delivery

You're likely going to have to deal with some furniture deliveries for your crib, dresser, glider, and other large items. Here are some tips on delivery and inspection.

White Glove: When purchasing a larger piece of furniture, you might have the option to upgrade to white glove delivery. White glove delivery means that instead of just leaving a giant box at your doorstep, the delivery company will bring it into your home, unpack it, assemble it, and remove the packaging (which is great for cribs). It is especially helpful for things like dressers or bookcases if your nursery is on a higher floor, since carrying furniture up the stairs is not easy. Make sure to budget for this in advance too—white glove delivery can be a few hundred dollars depending on the furniture item.

Damage: Open and inspect furniture right when it arrives. Things can break during shipment, or you may receive a defective product. If there is damage, including scuffs, broken hardware, or missing pieces, you can refuse the shipment or file a claim immediately. If you wait to open the box or don't report damage soon enough, the vendor may not take responsibility. If you see damage, always take detailed photos of the damaged areas as well as the outside of the shipping box.

assembly

If you decide to forgo white glove delivery and do most of the assembly yourself, here are some things you'll need to know.

- The crib should *always* be assembled inside the nursery. Most cribs are too big to fit through the door, and it's a huge pain to take them apart and reassemble!
- If you ordered any larger furniture, like a dresser, you'll need to be prepared to get it inside the room, which can be especially challenging if it's on a higher floor. I recommend removing all the drawers and bringing those up separately.
- Smaller items may require assembly as well, like a side table or lamp. Make sure to keep track of all the parts and directions and keep them with their corresponding item.
- You can always call in a professional (or even just a friend or family member) to help if you need it.

hiring professionals

If your project has major design elements, like custom built-ins, wallpaper, molding, etc., you may consider hiring a professional to help. You may not need (or want) to hire anyone at all, but if you do, it's good to know what to expect. Hiring contractors doesn't have to be as scary as it sounds if you are properly prepared. Here are some tips to help you have a good contracting experience.

- Start by asking family and friends for recommendations. If you don't have any luck there, try looking on Angie's List, Yelp, or other online services that offer user reviews.
- If possible, try to bundle the jobs. Instead of hiring an electrician, a painter, a wallpaper installer, and a handy man (or woman!), try to find contractors who are capable of multiple things so you can minimize the amount of people involved.
- Get multiple bids. You may be surprised to see how different quotes can be. Prepare yourself with a few different estimates so you can make an educated decision. If your top choice is the most expensive, they might be willing to match a competing bid.
- Only hire contractors with a valid license. It should be printed on their business card or website. If you are uncertain about a license, you can look up the Contractor's State Licensing Board in your state.
- Be specific with your instructions. Write a list of everything that you want done, and

include as many details as possible. For example, if you hire a painter, give them instructions on the exact color and finish of paint, note which walls to paint, and specify if they should paint the ceiling, molding, attached closet, etc. If you have high ceilings, let them know to bring a tall ladder. Go over the list with them to make sure they understand exactly what you want and come prepared with the right tools and materials.

- Never leave a contractor in your home unattended. You might also want to pop your head in every now and then to make sure everything is being done according to your instructions.

the order of things

When dealing with any job that involves contracting, there is a specific order in which things need to be done to avoid mistakes and extra costs.

Clear the Space: First and foremost, you'll have to clear the room. Move all existing furniture out of the room and, if needed, arrange for storage. See the next section for more on removing old items.

Evaluate: Take a good look around. Does your carpet need to be cleaned? Do you need to do any small repairs to drywall or baseboards? Make note of everything since you'll have contractors coming anyway.

Electrical: It might seem odd to start with electrical work, but if you're having wall sconces installed or a ceiling fixture cut in, you'll likely

moving things around a bit to see what works best.

Hang Heavy Items: If you have a heavy wall mirror, wall shelves, or a tricky piece of art, start with that. Heavy items should never be hung over a crib, and they should always be secured to the wall.

The Little Stuff: Finish up with the smaller things, like hanging pieces of art and wall hooks, and placing table lamps.

Add in Textiles: Lastly, put on your crib bedding, arrange any pillows, and throw a blanket on the glider.

Congratulate Yourself: You did it! Now sit back in that cozy glider and take in the sight of your new nursery!

your old stuff

Depending on what you used your nursery space for before, you may have old furniture or other items that need to be removed before you can bring all the new items in. You can of course store it if you have the space, but I also love to encourage my clients to donate these items. There are so many wonderful charities and organizations that accept furniture, décor, and even baby items. As we talked about in the Organization & Storage chapter, now is a good time to declutter anyway! See some of my favorite organizations and charities at the end of the book.

have to deal with drywall repair, which means you can't paint until after the repairs are complete.

Paint: After any drywall is repaired, you can paint the room. Use a low or zero VOC paint and don't forget to touch up the baseboards or crown moldings if needed.

Wall Treatments: After the paint is dry, you can install wallpaper or have a mural painted if you've included either in your design.

Window Treatments: It's generally good to hang curtains before artwork since curtains typically take up some wall space too. Just make sure you clean up any dust beforehand so the window treatments don't get dirty during installation.

Bring in Furniture: Bring in your large furniture pieces, and arrange them how you've planned in your floor plan. You might even try

Right: Customizable art by Cut Out & Co.

CHAPTER 12

Finishing Touches

Putting the finishing touches on your nursery will really take it to the next level. In this chapter, you'll learn how finishing touches can make all the difference, and how you can use styling to give your nursery a designer look.

Left: Malibu Diamond Pink pattern designed by Holli Zollinger

styling your nursery

Styling can mean the difference between a room that looks good and a room that looks great. It's what makes a room look pulled together, gives it personality, and makes it look real (not like a staged photo from a catalog). A blanket casually thrown over the glider, fresh cut flowers, a few curated books on a shelf. These are things that you don't necessarily immediately notice when you're looking at a room, but they are pleasing to the eye. For example, you may have heard that a lot of real estate agents and home stagers will place a bowl of lemons on the kitchen counter to make the home feel more inviting. It adds a pop of color, a focal point, and a "fresh" vibe.

Styling is of course important when photographing a space, but it's also something you can do in your nursery (or your home) just for yourself. Good styling makes a room feel warm and welcoming. The good news is that you don't even need to purchase any new items to style with—you can use what you already have!

my favorite styling tricks

There are some styling tricks for the nursery that I use time and time again—you might be able to spot them if you look back through the photos in this book!

Add Greenery: I love plants and fresh flowers in the nursery. They bring life and color into the space. You might be surprised how much of an impact plants can make. You can use faux plants too! Make sure to research first about the safety of certain plants in the

nursery as some are toxic to children and/or pets.

Display a Throw Blanket: Add a throw blanket to the glider, either over the arm or over the back. I like to choose a blanket that's made of a different material and color than the glider to add texture. If there's also an open storage bin in the room, I like to add some extra blankets in there to fill it out.

Showcase Your Books: Choose a few of your favorite baby books and display them on a shelf with a few other accessories. Books add color, interest, and personality to the room.

Add Sentimental Items: I always ask my clients if they have hand-me-downs or sentimental items that they want to include in the nursery. You can include a family photo in a cute frame, a vintage rattle, a knit pillow from Grandma—little touches that bring memories into the space.

Use Stuffed Animals: A well-placed stuffed animal looks adorable, a pile of twenty looks messy. When I'm shooting nurseries, I like to add just a few in certain spots. One on the glider, a few smaller ones on a bookcase or shelf, and maybe one in a storage basket with some blankets.

Decorative Pillows: You may see photos in this book that have pillows in the crib. This is *just* for decoration, but you can see how nice it looks. Just remember to remove them if you're putting the baby in the crib. Pillows also look nice on the glider, or even as a small pile on the floor.

Steam the Curtains: If you have curtains in your nursery, chances are they arrived folded and may still have wrinkles. Steaming or ironing the curtains will make the room feel so much more elegant.

Incorporate Your Favorite Items: Did you buy or receive a toy, piece of clothing, or other item that you just love? Put it on display! If you have wall hooks, hang up one of your favorite little outfits. Place that special toy on a shelf where you can see it. I like to encourage my clients to keep the things they love within eyesight.

Left top: Design by Ashley Joy Houston
Right: Steaming your curtains will make a huge difference!

move things around

There is no hard-and-fast rule about exactly how to place styling items. When I'm at a photoshoot, I will sometimes move an item a quarter inch several times until I'm satisfied with its exact placement—luckily I work with a very understanding photographer! This is why styling is so fun—you can constantly move the little details around and change up how the room looks without altering the design.

make a mess

Here's the thing—nurseries get messy. It just happens. So it may seem pointless to take the time to style the room if it's only going to get messed up. The great thing about styling is that it doesn't take a lot of time, so you can quickly put things back in place while you're doing your regular tidying up. It's also fun to change things up, so each time you are doing your cleaning, you can try a new arrangement of accessories or a different plant. Have fun!

the perfect photo

If you want to share your nursery with others, you'll want to get a great photo! Use the aforementioned styling tips to get the space in tip-top shape, and then use these tricks to get a great photo—no fancy camera required.

For this nursery, we styled four different items on the left of the crib. Each one gives the room a different feel.

Lighting: The most important aspect of getting a good photo, especially on a phone, is lighting. Natural lighting looks the best for interiors, so take the photo during the time of day where your nursery gets bright and even natural light.

Turn Off the Lights: It might seem counter-intuitive to turn off the lights for good lighting, but leaving lights on can cast a yellowish color on the photo and create odd shadows.

Take It Straight: Try to line up your camera so the edges of the furniture and walls all look straight. You can fix some of this in post-editing, but it's good to try to do as much with the camera as you can.

Choose Your Angles: When I'm shooting a nursery with my photographer, I like to take wide shots that show most of the room as well as detail shots. I like to have horizontal and vertical options for both as well so I can pick and choose when I'm editing. More is always better! Try some shots that are of a single wall, some shots of the corner, maybe even an upward shot of the chandelier. Play around with your camera and see what looks best.

Edit: Editing is super important in photography and can completely change the look of a photo. Just using a simple editing app on your phone can do so much! I usually edit photos to be a bit lighter and brighter, and crop them a little if necessary.

Designed by Elizabeth "Bitsie" Tulloch

CHAPTER 13

A Sustainable Nursery

We're lucky to live in a day and age where options are abundant. We have access to organic crib bedding, eco-friendly furniture, and non-toxic paints to keep our families safe. In addition to keeping chemicals out of our living space, we can work to reduce waste and better our environment.

Left: Herbal Study Light pattern designed by Holli Zollinger

Back in 2005, when I started design school, we had an entire course on environmental design. At the time, it was still pretty novel and I remember being shocked at some of the things I was learning. We really took a deep dive into the materials and processes that were used to manufacture fabric, rugs, furniture, paint, etc. We learned what risks we take by having these items in our homes. I have continued to do my own research ever since and have learned so much about not only what the risks are, but what we can do about them to keep our families and our planet safe.

breathe easy

"Eco," "green," and "natural" have become buzzwords in interior design and the baby industry, but that doesn't necessarily mean that things with this label are safer for your child. A lot of these terms are not regulated and can be confusing. When it comes down to it, you want what's going to be the safest for your baby. Here's what you need to know.

the dirt

The unfortunate reality is that every material and process involved in the creation of a piece of furniture, fabric, or décor has the risk of toxin exposure. Harmful chemicals can come from glues, varnishes, plastics, paints, stains, fibers, and fillings in addition to the potential pesticides and other toxins used in growing and harvesting natural materials. In today's world, it's almost impossible to avoid. The main way that these toxins and harmful chemicals get into our bodies is by breathing them into our lungs. Babies have very tiny and vulnerable lungs, so they are much more susceptible to toxin exposure than adults.

I always suggest to my clients that if they're going to invest in organic or "green" products, these are the best items to start with:

- Items that will be close to the baby's face, like a crib mattress, sheets, and rugs
- Items that may end up in your baby's mouth, like the top rail of the crib, bottle nipples, and pacifiers
- Items that linger in the air, like vapors from cleaning supplies

Right: Ceiling mural by Wall Art by Allyson

Artwork by Minted artist Stephanie Ryan

what you can do

You could spend a lifetime researching every chemical and possible side effect of every item in your home. But even if you did, that doesn't necessarily mean that you'd have the options (or budget) to replace everything with a better option. That's why I like to focus on a few changes that will make the biggest difference.

Organic Crib Mattresses: An organic crib mattress and mattress pad are a great place to start, and there are a lot of options available. Look for a mattress that's made with organic materials and that does not use any toxic chemicals in its production (both for the outside fabric of the mattress and the inside core material). Bear in mind that organic mattresses may be more expensive, so include this in your budget. Look for mattresses that are Greenguard certified and/or GOTS certified (Global Organic Textile Standard). See my favorite brands in the Shopping Guide.

Non-Toxic Finishes: Some babies like to chew on the crib rail when they are teething and can even ingest the finish. Look for furniture, especially the crib, with a non-toxic and water-based paint or finish. Another good feature to look for is furniture built out of hard-

If a manufacturer's website doesn't give you all the information you need, call and ask specifically what chemicals and processes are used. However, so much of this information is hidden or proprietary, even for employees, so you may not get a straight answer.

woods rather than particle board, which often contain chemical adhesives and even formaldehyde. Again, look for that Greenguard certification.

Organic Fabrics: Choosing organic fabrics for your crib bedding and baby clothing is a great idea, but options can be limited. You may find it difficult to find something that fits your color palette or theme. If that's the case, opt for organic crib sheets even if the bumper and skirt are not. The baby's face will be closest to the sheet. For fabrics, look for OEKO-TEX® certification and/or GOTS certification.

Air Filtration: You may consider getting an air filtration unit to keep in the nursery. A lot of parents do this to remove particles from the air that can act as irritants or allergens, but you can also remove some of the VOCs in the air with an activated carbon filter. Some filters are also dual-purpose and can be used as a fan or humidifier as well. Talk to your pediatrician before adding any humidity to the nursery.

Off-Gassing: Off-gassing is the release of chemicals into the air from products we have in our home. One of the best things you can do after your nursery design is done is to open up the windows and doors and let all the brand new items air out. Get rid of any plastic wrap or extra packaging, launder all the textiles that you can, and vacuum the rug several times.

Paint and wallpaper (especially vinyl based) also have potential for off-gassing, so always go with low or zero VOC paints and glues (VOC = Volatile Organic Compound). Don't bring anything into the nursery that has a perfume or fragrance, such as an air freshener or candle. These are often made with chemical fragrances that can off-gas continually.

Lingering Smells: If you purchase an item for your nursery that has a chemical smell when you open it, let that item off-gas either outside or in the garage until the smell is gone (sometimes this can take a few weeks if the smell is really strong). I also recommend washing everything that you can, even plastic toys, to remove as much chemical residue as possible.

PRO TIP

✔ In my experience, rugs can often have a chemical smell, especially if they are made of synthetic materials. Try this trick: lay it out, sprinkle baking soda over the entire rug, let it sit for a few hours (or even overnight), and then vacuum it several times. Sometimes this may need to be repeated.

around your home

Aside from furniture and décor, your baby can also be exposed to toxins via baby products, lotions, and cleaning products. Try to buy baby care and cleaning products that are made from natural ingredients so you won't have to worry. Any dangerous cleaning products or medicines should be stored completely out of baby's reach and locked up if possible. Check the EWG's Skin Deep® database for information on product ingredients.

plants

Having plants in the nursery is a great way to gently clean the air while also adding a beautiful design element. I love the way that plants bring life to a space! Before adding plants, do a little research to see which plants are safe around children and pets—some can be toxic or have sharp edges or points on the leaves. Place them in spots where they won't fall and if you're using real plants, use organic and non-toxic soil. Once your baby can crawl and pull up, you may need to remove any floor plants from the nursery.

reducing waste

Let's face it—the interior design industry uses a lot of resources. There's all the new furniture and décor, the transportation to ship it, all the packaging and boxes, pollution created by manufacturing, and even deforestation. Here are a few ways to cut down on the carbon footprint of designing your nursery.

Buy for Longevity: This is the most impactful decision you can make for the environ-

ment. Purchase items that you plan to keep for many years, especially furniture. Make sure you're buying quality pieces that aren't too trendy so you're sure to love them for years to come (this goes for all the rooms in your home!).

Buy Sustainable Materials: If your budget allows, try to purchase items made from solid wood that was sustainably harvested instead of MDF (look for an FSC® certification label).

Repurpose Items You Already Have: If you've got an old dresser in storage, or a few art pieces that never found a spot in your home, you can repurpose them! You can easily repaint or refinish furniture, switch out hardware to give it new life, reframe artwork, etc. Buying higher quality pieces also ensures that you can continue to repurpose things down the line.

Buy Used or Vintage Items: If you have a little time to dig around, you can find some great used and vintage pieces. However, I do not recommend this for cribs as they should be up to current safety standards. Previously owned items should also be thoroughly checked for structural integrity and safety, and for things like lead paint or toxic varnishes.

Save Boxes: If you're having a new baby, chances are you will be cleaning out areas of your home to make room. Hang on to the shipping boxes and use them to organize items to donate or throw out. You can break down boxes so they lay flat and slide them under a bed.

Donate Old Items: If you have items you need to get rid of to make room for the nursery, donate as much as possible so those items can be reused. There are even organizations that will come and pick up your items for free!

You can help reduce waste by reusing a piece you already own, or purchasing vintage. Designed by Elizabeth "Bitsie" Tulloch.

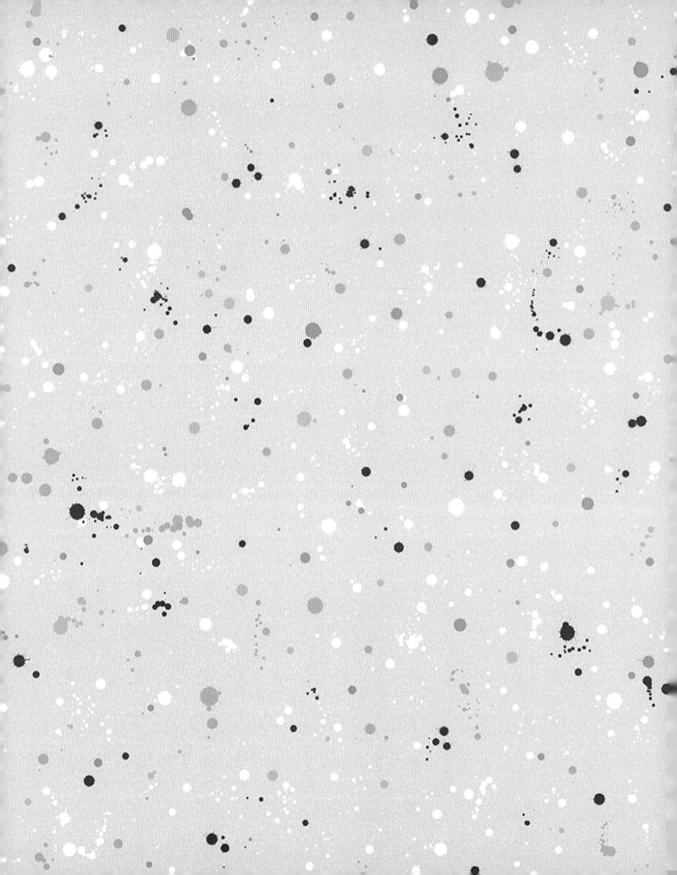

CHAPTER 14

Nursery Adaptations

No two families are alike, and sometimes there are special circumstances or surprises in life that make designing a nursery even more challenging.

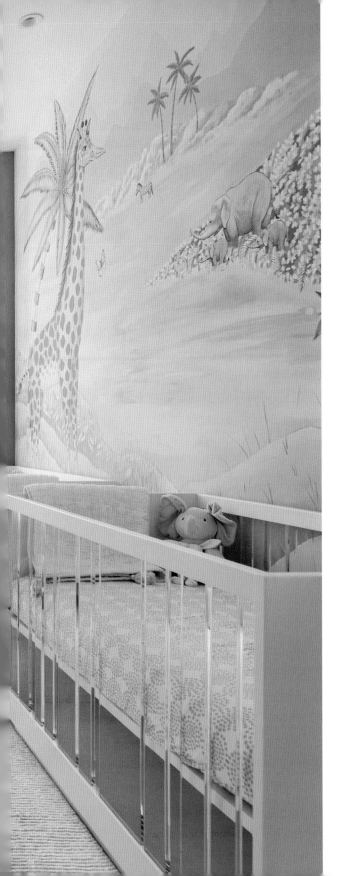

I've worked with hundreds of people on their nurseries over the years, and I've yet to meet two families that are identical. I've worked with people going through IVF, people who are adopting, people who are using a surrogate, single parents, LGBTQ+ parents, and the list goes on. I've worked on nursery designs for clients who are renting, or owning, or moving across the country.

We don't always get to decide how life leads us to parenthood, or how things go when we get there. Your particular circumstances may require a little more effort in some areas, and may be easier in others. Use the guide below to help you navigate through any particularly challenging circumstances.

This room has two cribs for twins and a wall mural to tie the whole space together. Designed by Patricia Tang Golumbic and Sam Simon, Mural by Sam Simon.

twins (or more!)

I've done lots of nurseries for twins over the years, and there are two main challenges: space and time. It's often tricky to fit two cribs in a nursery, so space can become an issue. Also, twins have a habit of arriving early, so your planning time can be cut short (see more on this in the next section).

- If you're having twins, yes, you will need two cribs. This is the biggest challenge since fitting two cribs safely in one room is often difficult. If you can fit two, make sure they are a safe distance apart (so they can't climb into the other crib). If you can't fit two, consider looking at mini crib options.
- Go back and look through the Small Nursery section in the Floor Plan chapter. Even if your room is a good size, you will have more furniture and more things to store, especially if you're having both a boy and a girl.

- If you have space, opt for a larger glider since you may be nursing or rocking two babies at once. You can even get a double-wide glider or a loveseat to allow space for you and potentially another person to help out at feeding and/or rocking time.
- If you put two cribs in the nursery, make sure to get a monitor system that will allow you to see both babies. Refer back to the Baby Monitor section of the Nursery Safety chapter.
- The same rules apply for triplets, just in threes instead of twos. Triplets have an even higher risk of arriving early, so try to get as much done early on as you can.

baby comes early

Regardless if you're having one baby, twins, or even triplets and beyond, babies are unpredictable and if you find yourself with your bundle of joy a bit earlier than expected, don't worry!

- Most babies will sleep in a co-sleeper or bassinet for the first three to five months, so it's okay if your furniture hasn't arrived yet. You can also use a changing pad on the floor or bathroom counter, or even just a portable changing pad until your dresser arrives.

- Focus on the essentials, like a place for baby to sleep and a safe car seat. Take care of baby and yourself first and the nursery will come together in its own time.

you're renting

Just because you rent instead of own doesn't mean you can't have a fabulous nursery. There are just a few extra guidelines you may have to follow. Depending on your lease, things like painting or wallpaper can require permission, so I find that it's usually best to contact the landlord or owner before you start work on the nursery to make sure they are okay with what you are planning.

- You may not be able to paint the walls, so choose a color scheme that works with the existing wall color.
- Removable or peel-and-stick wallpaper is a great option for renters too, since it has the look of wallpaper, but won't damage walls and is completely removable. It can also help cover up the walls if you don't like the existing color.
- Take extra care with installation. Because you need to be extra mindful about securing items to the walls, you may end up with larger holes if/when you move out. Be aware that you'll likely need to spackle and potentially touch-up those areas with paint if/when you leave.

Top: Be ready with a place for baby to sleep, even if it's just a bassinet or co-sleeper.
Bottom: Removable wallpaper is a great option for renters, since it peels right off the wall.

plans to move

I've had clients who were planning on moving into a new home shortly after having their baby, or knew that there was potential for them to need to move in the near future. If this is your case, there are a few design points to keep in mind.

- You'll probably want to stay away from adding things that are permanent, like wallpaper or a mural. These won't be able to come with you when you move, and can even affect the resale value of your home.
- Keep the paint scheme simple. If you're planning on moving in a few months, now might not be the time to paint the room a bright color since you may need to paint it back before you move.

- Invest in items that you can take with you, and that are versatile enough to reuse in a new space. For example, you may not want to invest too heavily in custom window treatments, since you will likely not be able to reuse them in a new home.

Don't skimp on safety. Even though you won't be there long, it's still important to make the nursery safe.

---

not finding out the sex of the baby

I once had a client who was having a baby boy, but wanted to have florals as part of the nursery design. I've also worked with dark blue in a girl's nursery, and incorporated lavender for a boy. The bottom line is that you don't have to stick to gender norms if you don't want to! If you are choosing not to learn the sex of your baby, or prefer the idea of a neutral space, there are certain design steps you can take.

- In the Color & Theme chapter, we talked a little bit about how you don't have to stick to gendered color expectations when designing your space. Any child can inhabit any space, so go with what you like!

- If you *do* want the nursery to reflect a more traditional vision of either a boy or a girl's room but you aren't finding out ahead of time, design most of the room as neutral as possible and then add in the more specific items after the baby is born. Choose artwork and décor that comes in multiple color options. Bookmark everything you like and, as soon as the baby is born, order everything in the appropriate color. Keep this list as small as possible so you won't have a lot of work to do once the baby is born.

double function

The nursery can often take over the room that used to be the guest room or office. If you still need that space to have a double function, things can certainly get interesting.

- The floor plan will be the trickiest part. If you need to fit a guest bed, look for a pull out, or something that can fold away to save space. For an office, look for a desk that's not too deep, or that can fold up against the wall.
- There are certain things that don't really have to happen in the actual nursery. You can change a baby on any surface, even on the floor. Maybe there's a spot elsewhere in your home that can be your makeshift changing station to free up some space in the nursery. Same goes for toys and books—those can be stored in another part of the home if necessary.

- If you have a guest over, you likely won't want to have baby sleeping in there with them. Make sure you have a plan for when the room needs to function as a guest room, office, etc. without the baby being present.

sharing with an older child

Not everyone will put the baby in their very own room. If your nursery is going to be shared by the baby and another child, you'll need to make a few adaptations.

- Prepare the older child for the new baby. Make sure they know that they are going to have to share their space, and go over some rules with them.
- The floor plan will be a challenge here as well since you'll likely need to include both a crib and a bed. Go back to the Floor Plan chapter and lay things out as best you can. If you can't fit both, look for a mini crib option. If possible, place the crib closer to the door so you can quickly pop in during the night without walking through the room and potentially waking up the other child.

- The overall design can be cohesive, but each child can still have individuality. For example, the basics of the room (paint, rug, furniture) can coordinate together, but each child may have their own bedding or décor pieces.
- Older children may have toys or other things that can be safety hazards for babies, like small toys with choking hazards. Go through all their items and remove anything that's unsafe and keep it in another room.

you're adopting

I've worked with lots of parents over the years who were adopting, both domestically and internationally. However, adoption does come with its own set of challenges when it comes to the nursery.

- You may not know the baby's age. Whether you're adopting locally or internationally, you may run into a situation where you don't know what the baby's exact age will be. In this situation, I recommend covering all the bases. It's good to have a crib ready no matter what since that can cover you from newborn all the way up to toddler.

- Some adoption agencies will require a home check to make sure that your home is safe and that you are prepared for the baby. Each agency may go about this a little differently, so get that information as soon as you can. Keep the nursery simple until all the papers are signed. This would be a great time to refer to that list of furniture essentials on page 58. You don't want to end up spending a lot of money on something and then finding out it needs to be removed.

- You may not know when the baby is going to arrive. Even with domestic private adoption, there's no guarantee that the baby will arrive when you think or hope it will. For this reason, I recommend making sure that you have a space for them, but again, keeping it very simple until everything is signed.

babies with disabilities or medical issues

Having a baby with a disability or a specific medical issue does not mean you can't still have a beautiful nursery. Depending on baby's needs, you just might have to make some adjustments for health and accessibility.

- The first thing I recommend is talking to your doctor about the specific medical and care needs that your baby will have. Will they need certain types of equipment at home?

- Once you know what you'll need, go back to the Floor Plan chapter and move things around to include any new necessary items.

- Keep the floor plan as open and accessible as possible. Function will be even more important in most situations, so you'll want to lay things out in a way that promotes easy access to everything you will need, and minimizes clutter.

Conclusion

One of my favorite parts of being a nursery designer is having the opportunity to work with each of my clients to build a space that represents so much more than just a place where baby can sleep. I get to see how excited they are when they show me their empty room, a blank slate, sharing with me all their hopes and dreams for the nursery—and their new little one. I get to see their face light up when the nursery is being installed, finally getting to see things come together. I've formed relationships with hundreds of moms, dads, parents, grandparents, and families over the years, and it brings me so much joy to be able to watch their families grow.

Having a beautiful, safe, comfortable nursery to begin your journey of parenthood can serve as the foundation for the memories you will make in the space. Parenthood is beautiful, and messy. That night-light you chose is what will light your way through countless sleepless nights; that glider is where you'll rock your baby, hoping they fall asleep soon (and stay asleep!); that ottoman is where you will put your feet up, if only for a moment.

The nursery is where you will wander sleepless in the night, clean all kinds of unsavory things, trip on toys, and cry when your baby hasn't stopped crying for hours. These moments are precious in their own way, and over time you'll learn to take it all in stride. Don't worry if your nursery isn't perfect, if something arrives late, or if the paint color turned out a couple shades darker than you hoped. Imperfection is woven into the fabric of parenthood! What makes a truly perfect nursery is the love, care, and attention you give that space in your home. Have fun with the design process, enjoy the creative venture, and try to let your worries take a back seat to the memories you will make with your family.

I sincerely hope that you've enjoyed reading this book, and also that you will enjoy every moment of creating a special space for your baby. We've gone through every aspect of design from initial inspiration to installation, and you have all the tools you need to create a beautiful, functional, and safe space all your own! You've learned about budgeting, choosing the right furniture, and lots and lots of safety tips. You can use the tools in this book to stay organized, on budget, and on schedule. I hope you feel empowered, confident, and ready to jump into your design.

Left: Tessa Scallop Rainbow pattern designed by Holli Zollinger

Shopping Guide

In all my years of nursery design, I have worked on more than 200 projects. I've visited with manufacturers, gone to the industry trade shows, and kept up on all the trends and safety standards in baby and child design. My clients trust me to source products that are beautiful, functional, and high quality, and I have a great database of brands I stand behind. Here, you will find my favorite brands, companies, websites, and places to shop!

All of the companies and brands listed in this resource guide are brands that I have personally chosen to be included. I've worked with thousands of companies during my career and I definitely have favorite retailers, brands, and shops that I routinely use because of their great style and quality.

Left: Seville Garden Light pattern designed by Holli Zollinger

nursery furniture

AFK Furniture	www.afkfurniture.com	Million Dollar Baby	www.milliondollarbabyco.com
Babyletto	www.babyletto.com	Oeuf	www.oeufnyc.com
bloom	www.bloombaby.com	Pottery Barn Kids	www.potterybarnkids.com
Bratt Decor	www.brattdecor.com	Project Nursery	www.projectnursery.com
Crate & Kids	www.crateandkids.com	Romina Furniture	www.rominafurniture.com
ducduc	www.ducducnyc.com	Serena & Lily	www.serenaandlily.com
Franklin & Ben	www.franklinandben.com	Spot on Square	www.spotonsquare.com
Kalon Studios	www.kalonstudios.com	Stokke	www.stokke.com
Little Seeds	www.littleseedskids.com	Restoration Hardware	
Newport Cottages	www.newportcottages.com	Baby & Child	www.RHbabyandchild.com
Nursery Works	www.nurseryworks.net	Target	www.target.com
Milk Street Baby	www.milkstreetbaby.com	West Elm	www.westelm.com

crib mattresses

Avocado	www.avocadogreenmattress.com	Newton Baby	www.newtonbaby.com
Babyletto	www.babyletto.com	Nook	www.nooksleep.com
Colgate	www.colgatekids.com	Oeuf	www.oeufnyc.com
Naturepedic	www.naturepedic.com		

accent furniture

AFK Furniture	www.afkfurniture.com	Pottery Barn Kids	www.potterybarnkids.com
Anthropologie	www.anthropologie.com	Project Nursery	www.projectnursery.com
Crate & Kids	www.crateandkids.com	Restoration Hardware	
Goodee	www.goodeeworld.com	Baby & Child	www.RHbabyandchild.com
Jungalow	www.jungalow.com	Serena & Lily	www.serenaandlily.com
Lulu & Georgia	www.luluandgeorgia.com	Target	www.target.com
Modshop	www.modshop1.com	West Elm	www.westelm.com

gliders & rockers

Babyletto	www.babyletto.com	Oilo Studio	www.oilostudio.com
Best Home Furnishings	www.besthf.com	Pottery Barn Kids	www.potterybarnkids.com
Crate & Kids	www.crateandkids.com	Restoration Hardware	
ducduc	www.ducducnyc.com	Baby & Child	www.RHbabyandchild.com
Little Crown Interiors	www.littlecrowninteriors.com	Serena & Lily	www.serenaandlily.com
Lulu & Georgia	www.luluandgeorgia.com	Target	www.target.com
Monte Design	www.montedesign.com	West Elm	www.westelm.com
Nursery Works	www.nurseryworks.net		

art & décor

The Animal Print Shop	www.theanimalprintshop.com	Minted	www.minted.com
Anthropologie	www.anthropologie.com	Oliver Gal	www.olivergal.com
Artfully Walls	www.artfullywalls.com	Oopsy Daisy	www.oopsydaisy.com
Crate & Kids	www.crateandkids.com	Pottery Barn Kids	www.potterybarnkids.com
Etsy	www.etsy.com	Project Nursery	www.projectnursery.com
Goodee	www.goodeeworld.com	Restoration Hardware	
Gray Malin	www.graymalin.com	Baby & Child	www.RHbabyandchild.com
Leslee Mitchell	www.lesleemitchellart.com	Society6	www.society6.com
Lulu & Georgia	www.luluandgeorgia.com	Target	www.target.com

paint, wallpaper & decals

Anewall	www.anewall.com	Little Crown Interiors	www.littlecrowninteriors.com
Anthropologie	www.anthropologie.com	Lovely Wall Co.	www.thelovelywall.com
Carter & Main	www.carterandmain.com	Project Nursery	www.projectnursery.com
Cavern	www.cavernhome.com	Rebel Walls	www.rebelwalls.com
Clare Paint	www.clare.com	Spoonflower	www.spoonflower.com
Etsy	www.etsy.com	Tempaper	www.tempaperdesigns.com
Hygge & West	www.hyggeandwest.com	Urban Walls	www.uwdecals.com
Juju Papers	www.jujupapers.com		

lighting

Anthropologie	www.anthropologie.com	Restoration Hardware	
Bellacor	www.bellacor.com	Baby & Child	www.RHbabyandchild.com
Brite Lite	www.britelitetribe.com	Sazerac Stitches	www.sazeracstitches.com
Crate & Kids	www.crateandkids.com	Schoolhouse Electric	www.schoolhouse.com
I Lite 4 U	www.ilite4u.com	Serena & Lily	www.serenaandlily.com
Jungalow	www.jungalow.com	Shades of Light	www.shadesoflight.com
Lamps Plus	www.lampsplus.com	Stray Dog Designs	www.straydogdesigns.com
Lucent Lightshop	www.lucentlightshop.com	Target	www.target.com
Pottery Barn Kids	www.potterybarnkids.com	West Elm	www.westelm.com

crib bedding

Aden + Anais	www.adenandanais.com	Little Unicorn	www.littleunicorn.com
Anthropologie	www.anthropologie.com	New Arrivals, Inc	www.newarrivalsinc.com
Caden Lane	www.cadenlane.com	Oilo Studio	www.oilostudio.com
Carousel Designs	www.babybedding.com	Olli + Lime	www.olliandlime.com
Crate & Kids	www.crateandkids.com	Pottery Barn Kids	www.potterybarnkids.com
Kindred Kid & Baby	www.kindredkidandbaby.com	Project Nursery	www.projectnursery.com

Restoration Hardware		Spearmint Love	www.spearmintlove.com
Baby & Child	www.RHbabyandchild.com	Target	www.target.com
Serena & Lily	www.serenaandlily.com		

window treatments

Barn & Willow	www.barnandwillow.com	Pottery Barn Kids	www.potterybarnkids.com
Crate & Kids	www.crateandkids.com	Restoration Hardware	
Decoratd	www.decoratd.com	Baby & Child	www.RHbabyandchild.com
Half Price Drapes	www.halfpricedrapes.com	The Shade Store	www.theshadestore.com
Little Crown Interiors	www.littlecrowninteriors.com	Target	www.target.com
Loom Décor	www.loomdecor.com	West Elm	www.westelm.com

area rugs

Annie Selke	www.annieselke.com	Pottery Barn Kids	www.potterybarnkids.com
Anthropologie	www.anthropologie.com	Restoration Hardware	
Crate & Kids	www.crateandkids.com	Baby & Child	www.RHbabyandchild.com
Kroma Carpets	www.kromacarpets.com	Rug Studio	www.rugstudio.com
Lorena Canals	www.lorenacanals.com	Ruggable	www.ruggable.com
Lulu & Georgia	www.luluandgeorgia.com	West Elm	www.westelm.com

accessories & utility

Crate & Kids	www.crateandkids.com	Skip Hop	www.skiphop.com
Pottery Barn Kids	www.potterybarnkids.com	Target	www.target.com
Project Nursery	www.projectnursery.com	Ubbi	www.ubbiworld.com

plants & planters

Afloral	www.afloral.com	Planterina	www.planterina.com
Bloomscape	www.bloomscape.com	The Sill	www.thesill.com
Nearly Natural	www.nearlynatural.com	Target	www.target.com

toys

Crate & Kids	www.crateandkids.com	Pottery Barn Kids	www.potterybarnkids.com
Darling Clementine	www.darlingclementineshop.com	Target	www.target.com
Odin Parker	www.odinparker.com	Rose & Rex	www.roseandrex.com

safety

CPSC (Consumer Product Safety Commission)
www.cpsc.gov
EWG (Environmental Working Group)
www.ewg.org
FCS (Forest Stewardship Council)
www.fsc.org
GOTS (Global Organic Textile Standard)
www.global-standard.org
Greenguard
www.greenguard.org

IAFCS (International Association for Child Safety)
www.iafcs.org
JPMA (Juvenile Products Manufacturers Association)
www.jpma.org
OEKO-TEX
www.oeko-tex.com
Project Nursery
www.projectnursery.com
Target
www.target.com

registering

Babylist   www.babylist.com

Gugu Guru   www.guguguru.com

causes to support

A Sense of Home   www.asenseofhome.org
Baby2Baby   www.baby2baby.org
The Dad Gang   www.thedadgang.com
Every Mother Counts   www.everymothercounts.org
Foster More   www.fostermore.org

Sister Song   www.sistersong.net
Together We Rise   www.togetherwerise.org

Design & Photo Credits

All photographs are by David Casas and designs are by Little Crown Interiors unless otherwise noted below.

Acknowledgments

This book has been years in the making. I started writing it back in 2014, but didn't have the confidence or know-how to pursue it at that time. Several years later, I met Kyle Rutkin, who encouraged me to write a proposal and try to get this thing published. As a writer himself, his input and insight were invaluable, and his steadfast enthusiasm balanced my fear and imposter syndrome. Kyle, thank you for holding me accountable and (gently) pushing me to succeed!

A huge thanks to all of my amazing clients who let me into your homes to design your nurseries. Without you all, this wouldn't be possible. Each of you brought me such a unique experience and I learned from every single project. Thank you for allowing me into your lives, letting me meet your children, and trusting me with your nursery.

To David Casas, my photographer and friend of more than twenty years, thank you for every photoshoot where you crammed into a closet, laid on the floor, or crouched in a corner to get the perfect shot. Thank you for dealing with me every time I wanted to move something a quarter inch and shoot it again, and for providing this book with so many gorgeous images.

Thank you to the other designers and DIYers who let me use photos of their work in this book. There is so much talent out there in the world, and I'm grateful to be part of a design community who supported this book from the beginning.

To all of the contractors, workrooms, and vendors who made my designs a reality—you put your literal sweat into each of my projects to ensure they were installed perfectly, provided beautiful pieces of furniture, built my custom creations, sewed window treatments, painted walls, and installed wallpaper. Thank you for bringing my designs to life!

To my parents, thank you for supporting my artistic dreams from a young age. You encouraged me to be creative and supported my decision to become an interior designer. I have so many memories of working with Dad in the garage, helping him choose carpet for the living room, and making drawings so Mom could realize the vision. I have no doubt that those experiences shaped the person I am today. You also gave me my first nursery, with pastel floral wallpaper, and made the very smart decision to not let me paint my whole room black in my teenage years. Thanks, Mom and Dad!

To my boss at my very first design job fresh out of design school, I was inexperienced and eager to learn, and you taught me so much with kindness, even when I made mistakes (which I definitely did).

To my business partner for the first seven years of Little Crown Interiors, you taught me everything I know about babies, children, and parenthood, and so much of what I know about business and marketing. I wouldn't be where I am today without you and your beautiful family!

A huge thank you to my agent, Sharon Pelletier, and my editor, Hannah Robinson, for believing in this project. Both of you have been so supportive and have led me through this process with kindness and professionalism, even when I emailed lists of all the hundreds of questions I had. Thank you for taking a chance on this book, and for making it a wonderful experience for me!

To everyone at Simon & Schuster and Tiller Press, thank you for working to make this book become a reality. It takes a whole team of people to make a book, and I couldn't have asked for a better team.

To Dr. Ted Yoo, you listened to me every time I was frustrated or stressed, and gave me advice when I needed to bounce ideas around. You always challenge me to think in new ways, and you tell me the truth when I need to hear it. Thank you for supporting not just my work, but me.

Finally, thank you to all my friends and family who have been there with me throughout this project, from the very beginning. You celebrated with me when I found out this book was going to happen, and you supported me when I disappeared into a writing hole for weeks. You served as my test audience, gave me valuable opinions, and listened when I complained about how hard writing a book is (it's hard). I love you all!

About the Author

NAOMI COE founded Little Crown Interiors in 2008, and she has been designing nurseries and children's rooms for more than a decade. Bringing together beauty, functionality, and safety, Naomi believes in creating spaces for her clients that are unique, intentional, and curated. Her work has been featured widely in print, web, and on television including *Domino*, *HGTV*, *People Magazine*, *California Home & Design Magazine*, and many more. She lives in Southern California and works with clients all across the United States. Her home is full of plants, rocks and minerals, and paintings from her art school days.